NORTH AMERICAN LABOR MARKETS

COMMISSION FOR LABOR COOPERATION
NORTH AMERICAN AGREEMENT ON LABOR COOPERATION (NAALC)

North American Labor Markets

A Comparative Profile

COMMISSION FOR LABOR COOPERATION
NORTH AMERICAN AGREEMENT ON LABOR COOPERATION (NAALC)

Co-published by Bernan Press and the Commission for Labor Cooperation

Secretariat of the Commission for Labor Cooperation
One Dallas Centre
350 North St. Paul Street
Suite 2424
Dallas, TX 75201-4240 USA

www.naalc.org
214.754.1100
fax 214.754.1199

Distributed by
Bernan Associates
4611-F Assembly Drive
Lanham, MD 20706-4391 USA

www.bernan.com
800.274.4447
fax 800.865.3450

ISBN (English): 0-89059-070-2
ISBN (French): 0-89059-074-5
ISBN (Spanish): 0-89059-075-3

Acknowledgments

The Secretariat acknowledges the assistance of the following agencies:
— **United States:** The Bureau of International Labor Affairs, the Bureau of Labor Statistics, the Bureau of Economic Analysis, and the Bureau of the Census.
— **Canada:** Statistics Canada and Human Resources Development Canada.
— **Mexico:** The Ministry of Labor and Social Welfare (STPS) and the National Institute of Statistics, Geography, and Informatics (INEGI).
— The National Administrative Offices of the three NAALC parties.

The authors of this report are Joanne Steinberg and Maria-Elena Vicario. Additional assistance was provided by the staff of the Secretariat.

The authors would like to thank the following people for their invaluable comments on this report:
— Dr. Francisco Alba, El Colegío de México
— Dr. Gordon Betcherman, Ekos Research
— Dr. Richard Chaykowski, Queen's University
— Valerie Clements, Human Resources Development Canada
— Bob Cleveland, U.S. Bureau of the Census
— Dr. Elizabeth Dickson, Organisation for Economic Co-operation and Development
— Dra. Brigida García, Colegío de México
— Act. Francisco Javier Gutiérrez Guzman, INEGI
— Dr. Steven Herztenberg, Keystone Research Center
— Thea Lee, Economic Policy Institute
— Brenda Lipsett, Human Resources Development Canada
— Dr. Constantino Lluch, Organisation for Economic Co-operation and Development
— Dr. Michael J. Piore, Massachusetts Institute of Technology
— Dr. Carlos Salas, Universidad Nacional Autónomo de México
— Greg Schoepfle, Bureau of International Labor Affairs
— Constance Sorrentino, Bureau of Labor Statistics
— Dr. Paul Swaim, Organisation for Economic Co-operation and Development

Secretariat Staff:
— John McKennirey, Executive Director
— Dolores Ozuna, Executive Assistant
— Lance Compa, Director of Labor Law and Economics Research
— Eric Griego, International Labor Advisor
— Dr. Dalil Maschino, Senior Economist
— Joanne Steinberg, International Labor Advisor
— Maria-Elena Vicario, Senior Economist

—Dr. Leoncio Lara-Saenz, Director of Cooperation and Evaluations
—Alfredo Hernández, International Cooperative Activities Coordinator
—Penny Miller, Graphics Applications Specialist
—Marcelle Saint-Arnaud, Documentation Coordinator
—Dolores Simms, Financial Officer
—John Vincent, Manager of Operations

The Labor Secretariat of the Commission for Labor Cooperation is solely responsible for the contents of this report. Nothing in this report necessarily reflects the views of the Council of Ministers, of any government agency, or of any contractor who provided research assistance.

Contents

List of Tables

List of Figures

Chapter I: Economic and Social Context

Chapter II: The Changing Employment Landscape

The Evolution of Employment

Working Time and Nonstandard Work

The Knowledge-Driven Labor Market: A Higher Premium for Education and Skills

Unionization in North America

Chapter III: Employment Security Issues: Multiple Dimensions of Unemployment, Underemployment, and Job Insecurity

Chapter IV: Earnings, Productivity, Income Distribution, and Employment Benefits

Trends in Earnings

Trends in Productivity: Hourly Compensation Costs, Labor Productivity, and Unit Labor Costs in Manufacturing

Trends in Income Distribution

Executive Summary

This comparative profile of labor markets in North America is the first report of the international Secretariat of the Commission for Labor Cooperation. The Secretariat was established under the North American Agreement on Labor Cooperation, a supplementary accord to the North American Free Trade Agreement (NAFTA). The profile was initiated by the Council of Labor Ministers of Canada, Mexico, and the United States.

Economic and Social Context

The differing economic and social environments in Canada, Mexico, and the United States are reflected in the evolution of each country's labor market. In general, labor markets in Canada and the United States show many similarities, whereas Mexico's labor market is often different, in part because Mexico is a developing country. However, despite some notable differences, labor market trends in all three countries are similar in many respects, and trends transcend national borders.

Averages are becoming less and less relevant to describe the North American worker. Such averages mask the polarizations occurring in terms of hours of work, types of work, earnings, and income distribution. They also mask differences by age and gender. It is becoming increasingly important to disaggregate these variables to develop more accurate portraits of the three labor markets.

Several major shifts in the way North Americans work emerge from this review of the labor markets in Canada, Mexico, and the United States in 1984–1995. These shifts are highlighted below.

The Changing Employment Landscape

The labor force in Canada and the United States is characterized by a slowdown in growth, mainly attributable to the decreased participation of men and slower growth in the participation of women. In contrast, Mexico's labor force is growing very rapidly, fueled by a large, young population, as well as by an influx of women into the labor force and by growth in participation by men. The growth in male participation reflects the need to work to make up for declining incomes. Even this rapid growth is slower than it was in the late 1980s because of the slower population growth.

The labor force participation of women increased in all three countries during 1984–1995, with Mexico showing the fastest rate of increase. In 1995, women made up 46 percent of the U.S.

labor force, 45 percent of the Canadian labor force, and 32 percent of the Mexican labor force.

Mexican workers are significantly younger than their U.S. and Canadian counterparts. Proportionately, Mexico has almost twice the proportion of young people between the ages of 15 and 24 in the labor force (29 percent of the Mexican labor force).

Mexico experienced the highest rate of employment growth in North America during 1984–1995, twice as fast as in the United States and Canada. This rate was mainly the result of rapid growth in the informal sector. In all three countries, annual growth rates slowed over this period.

Throughout North America as well as globally, employment shares have shifted from the primary (farming, forestry, and fishing) and industry (mining, manufacturing, and construction) sectors to the service sector. Between 1984 and 1995, North America's working population shifted from 70 percent to 75 percent in services, from 20 percent to 17 percent in industry, and from 10 percent to 8 percent in the primary sector. The service sector accounted for more than 90 percent of employment growth over the period in all three countries.

This sectoral shift is also reflected in changes in the occupational structure of employment. Employment in managerial, technical, and professional occupations increased most rapidly in Canada and the United States, while employment in sales occupations increased most rapidly in Mexico. In all three countries, employment in processing occupations (production, craft, repair, operators, fabricators, and laborers) and primary occupations declined.

Wage and salary workers are the most common group in North America. While this group represented more than 80 percent of workers in Canada and the United States, it represented less than 60 percent of workers in Mexico. Mexico has a significantly higher proportion of self-employed and unpaid workers, many of whom work in the agricultural sector, compared with its North American partners. Most workers in Canada and the United States work for firms with more than 500 employees. In contrast, in Mexico, most workers are employed by firms with fewer than 15 employees. The greater proportion of self-employed and unpaid workers and of workers in small firms in Mexico is indicative of that country's larger informal employment sector.

Most North American workers still have a single full-time, paid job of indeterminate duration. However, the relative size of this group is declining. Nonstandard employment, including part-time workers, "own-account" self-employed workers (i.e., those with no employees), temporary or contract workers, and multiple job holders, is becoming more prevalent throughout North America and in many other member countries of the Organisation for Economic Co-operation and Development (OECD).

The predominant form of nonstandard employment in all three countries was part-time work. However, in Mexico, own-account self-employment was also very common. In all three countries, most nonstandard employment is in the service sector while a higher share of nonstandard work is performed by women and younger workers. The growth in nonstandard employment is reflected in changes in work hours. A smaller proportion of North Americans work a standard 40- to 48-hour week; a larger proportion is working either shorter or longer hours.

The skill levels of the North American work force are rising, and employment growth in higher-skill occupations is outstripping growth in lower-skill occupations in Canada and the United States. Mexico has a higher level of low-skill and medium-skill employment than Canada and the United States, but Mexican education and skill levels have improved considerably over the past decade.

It is also becoming increasingly evident that a growing polarization of the North American labor market is based on education and skill. Workers who are more educated and have higher skill levels tend to hold better-paying, more stable jobs. Workers who do not have the necessary education and skill levels experience higher levels of unemployment and underemployment in Canada and the United States. Conversely, in Mexico, unemployment rates for more-educated workers are higher, while less-educated workers must work to maintain their subsistence. Lower-skilled workers are receiving fewer training opportunities in the workplace than are their more skilled counterparts in all three countries.

Workers in the service sector, in larger firms, in higher-skill occupations, and with higher incomes have greater access to formal workplace training. Workers with lower education and skill levels are seeing their earnings deteriorate in all three countries.

Unionization rates in Canada and Mexico, above 30 percent, are substantially higher than rates in the United States. It is important to note that unionization rates in Mexico are calculated based on wage and salary workers who represent 59 percent of employment, compared with 88 percent and 84 percent of employment in the United States and Canada, respectively. Unionization rates have remained relatively stable in Canada and Mexico, while unionization declined significantly in the United States during 1984–1995—from 18.8 to 15 percent. One reason for Canada's relatively stable unionization rates is successful union organization efforts in the service sector, particularly in public services. Mexico's higher unionization rates compared with those of the United States are due to high rates in larger manufacturing establishments, the public sector, and state-run enterprises.

In both Canada and the United States, a greater percentage of union members are now in "white collar" occupations than in "blue collar" occupations. Unionized workers have aged over the past decade compared with all wage and salary workers. In all three countries there has been growth in categories of workers less prone to unionize, such as those in nonstandard employment and those excluded from legal protections for organizing.

Employment Security Issues

Unemployment, underemployment, and job insecurity have been of major concern in North America as well as globally. In 1995, unemployment in OECD countries amounted to 34.5 million people, or 7.6 percent of the OECD labor force—3 million more than in 1983. The overall unemployment level in North America dropped from 11.0 million workers in 1984 to 10.5 million workers in 1995, and the unemployment rate decreased from 7.4 percent to 5.8 percent over this period. This drop was mainly due to a decrease in the unemployment rate in the United States. The unemployment rate in Canada decreased during 1984–1989 and rose higher than the U.S. rate between 1990 and 1992, after which it eased slowly downward. The unemployment rate in Mexico declined between 1984 and 1991 and rose between 1992 and 1994. The Mexican unemployment rate rose sharply in 1995 because of the economic crisis.

Canada had the highest unemployment rate in North America during 1984–1995, followed by the United States and Mexico. Mexican unemployment rates are comparatively low because most workers must work to maintain their subsistence, in part because they do not have unemployment insurance. All three countries use internationally accepted criteria for measuring unemployment. Some of the difference in unemployment rates between Canada and the United States can be explained by the fact that "passive" job hunters (such as those who read only help-wanted advertisements) are considered unemployed in Canada and are not in the labor force in the United States.

Unemployment rates among young people (under 25 years of age) in 1995 were more than double those of other workers in North America. However, young workers in other OECD countries have higher unemployment rates than in North America.

The proportion of workers who become unemployed because they lose their jobs has grown in all three countries since 1988. Mexico and Canada have a larger proportion of such unemployed workers than does the United States; more unemployed workers are labor force reentrants in the United States than in Canada.

The incidence of unemployment in North America (or the people in the labor force who become unemployed in a given period) is high. In Canada, 24 percent of the labor force was unemployed at some point in 1993, compared with 15 percent of the U.S. labor force in the same year and 15–20 percent of the Mexican labor force in 1991. This high incidence of unemployment may contribute to the sense of job insecurity felt in North America. Furthermore, more than one out of five jobs in North America lasts for one year or less—a significantly higher ratio than in other OECD countries. This figure suggests that there is more churning and less job stability in North America compared to other OECD countries.

There has been a rise in other forms of labor market slack such as involuntary part-time employment, discouraged workers who give up looking for work, workers who work fewer than 15 hours per week, and those who take low-wage work. The relative importance of each of these indicators varies significantly in each country in North America.

Earnings, Productivity, Income Distribution, and Benefits

During 1984–1995, real average weekly earnings for wage and salary workers in the private formal sector declined in Mexico. In Canada real earnings at the national level stagnated during this period, as did real earnings for full-time wage and salary workers in the United States. In all three countries, labor productivity grew. The real minimum wage in Mexico and the United States declined substantially; however, the percentage of minimum-wage workers was considerably reduced throughout 1984–1995. Women occupied a higher share of minimum-wage jobs in all three countries,

although gender differences narrowed during this period.

Throughout North America, there is a wide dispersion of earnings among sectors. Workers in social services and retail trade had the lowest real earnings of all sectors. Earnings in finance, insurance, and real estate grew the most. Real earnings in the manufacturing sector declined in the United States and Mexico and increased slightly in Canada.

Inequality in total household income distribution after taxes and after transfers has increased in both the United States and Mexico, and family or individual income inequality has decreased slightly in Canada. Nevertheless, in North America overall, more households are moving toward higher levels of income. In Canada and to a lesser extent in the United States, growing income inequality has partially been offset by social transfers and more progressive taxation to redistribute income.

The three countries have significantly different legislated programs covering employment benefits. In Mexico, such benefits are available to about one-third of the labor force (those enrolled in the social security system), whereas in Canada and the United States, more than 80 percent of the labor force is eligible for most legislated benefits. In all three countries, benefits are gaining greater importance as a form of compensation and their costs are growing relative to wages and salaries. Benefit costs have continued to rise in all three countries as the population of older workers grows, particularly in Canada and the United States, and as demand rises for health care services and pensions. In addition, the distribution of benefits among workers is being altered as growing numbers of workers in nonstandard arrangements receive reduced or no employment benefits. As profit-sharing and other benefit mechanisms grow in popularity, the forms of benefits and their relative importance are changing.

Introduction

In January 1994 the North American Agreement on Labor Cooperation (NAALC), a supplementary accord to the North American Free Trade Agreement (NAFTA), came into force. The NAALC is the first agreement that links labor rights and labor standards to an international trade agreement. Through this agreement, the continental trading partners seek to improve working conditions and living standards, and they commit themselves to promoting 11 labor principles to protect, enhance, and enforce basic rights of workers.

The NAALC established the Commission for Labor Cooperation, consisting of a governing Council of Labor Ministers in the United States, Mexico, and Canada, and an international Secretariat of the Commission for Labor Cooperation, located in Dallas, Texas. The NAALC assigns to the Secretariat the responsibility (among others) of preparing reports on "labor market conditions such as employment rates, average wages, and labor productivity." This assignment responds to one of the central objectives of the NAALC: "to encourage publication and exchange of information, data development and coordination, and joint studies to enhance mutually beneficial understanding of the laws and institutions governing labor in each Party's territory."

This is the first of the Secretariat's labor reports. The Secretariat is also preparing a companion report that compares the labor laws in the three countries. The aim of both reports is to promote a broader understanding of North American labor matters, using a practical and accessible comparative format.

This comparative profile is meant to serve as a statistical handbook of comparable labor market data for the three countries, including limited commentary on trends and comparability issues. The Secretariat has worked with the labor agencies of the three countries—the United States Bureau of Labor Statistics, Human Resources Development Canada, and the Mexican Secretariat of Labor and Social Welfare—to assemble a comprehensive, side-by-side presentation of labor market statistics. The statistics presented are official government data from the Mexican Institute of Statistics, Geography, and Informatics; the U.S. Bureau of Labor Statistics; and Statistics Canada. The statistics are at the national level, unless otherwise indicated. Wherever possible, information has been broken out by age, gender, and education level to indicate the significance of these fundamental factors.

Considerable effort was made to assemble comparable data for the three countries. However, exact comparability was not always possible because of differences in statistical approaches and methodologies and in data availability among the three countries. With a few exceptions, as noted in the text, the data were not harmonized. Comparability issues are discussed in each chapter's overview.

The profile will be produced regularly to provide up-to-date information and to facilitate research efforts over time. This first edition compares economic and social characteristics of the North American labor market during 1984–1995. This period was selected for two reasons. First, it spans several years before implementation of both the United States–Canada Free Trade Agreement and the NAFTA as a basis for comparison. Second, all three countries had recovered from earlier recessions and had strong economic growth in 1984 compared with the preceding two years.

Chapter I of this report gives a statistical description of the broad economic and social characteristics of each country—including macroeconomic, demographic, and labor force indicators—as a backdrop for the comparative analysis.

Chapter II examines the changing employment landscape during 1984–1995, including employment growth patterns; changes in the sectoral, occupational, and structural composition of employment; the growth in nonstandard work and changes in hours of work; shifts in the education and training of the work force; and changes in the structure of unionized employment in North America.

Chapter III deals with employment security issues facing North America, including unemployment and underemployment, and it looks at such complementary indicators as discouraged workers, workers who earn the minimum wage or less, and job tenure and flux.

Chapter IV reports on trends in earnings, productivity, income distribution, and benefits, including the trend toward increased polarization over the past decade.

Appendix A suggests ways to improve data comparability. Appendix B provides statistical tables of selected annual indicators during 1984–1995.

In addition to regular updates of this profile, the Secretariat plans to produce special analytical reports that will attempt to explore, in more depth, the social and economic impacts of selected labor market trends and to identify the factors that underlie those trends.

Economic and Social Context

Overview

The three North American countries account for a relatively small percentage of the world's population (close to 7 percent in 1995). However, North America has the strongest regional economy in the world. The North American gross domestic product (GDP) represented 31 percent of the world's GDP in 1995.[1]

The recent global trend toward more liberalized trade policies has brought about new regional and multilateral trade agreements. In North America, Mexico joined the General Agreement on Tariffs and Trade in 1986, Canada and the United States implemented the bilateral Free Trade Agreement in 1988, and all three countries implemented the North American Free Trade Agreement (NAFTA) in 1994. The region is a powerful trading block, generating 17 percent of world merchandise exports and 21 percent of world merchandise imports in 1995.

Table 1 presents a snapshot of North America in 1995. It shows where Canada, Mexico, and the United States stood with regard to a number of economic and social indicators, some of which are discussed below in a global context.

In addition to more liberalized trade, several significant changes have affected world labor markets during 1984–1995. The proportion of the working-age population in the labor force in countries belonging to the Organisation for Economic Co-operation and Development (OECD) has continued to grow, mainly because of increased female participation rates. The North American labor force has grown more rapidly than in OECD countries, at an average annual rate of 1.9 percent during 1984–1993 compared with 1.1 percent in all OECD countries during 1983–1993. The labor force participation rate in North America is also higher than in European OECD countries—74.9 percent compared with 66.8 percent in 1995.[2] The North American labor force accounted for 13 percent of the world's labor force in 1993.

Another important change is the shift in the composition of employment in both developed and developing countries. Employment in the primary sector (agriculture, forestry, and fishing) has declined, the relative importance of industry employment has diminished, and employment in the service sector has risen dramatically. The International Labor Organization estimated that between 1965 and 1991, the structure of the world's working population shifted from 57 percent to 48 percent in agriculture, from 19 to 17 percent in industry, and from 24 percent to 35 percent in services.[3] In North America, the structure

The North American labor force has grown more rapidly than in OECD countries.

Table 1

Table 1

North America in 1995: Labor Indicators

Indicators	Canada	Mexico	United States
GDP (billions U.S.$)	$566	$252	$6,743
GDP per Capita[a] (U.S.$)	$20,401	$7,239	$25,512
GDP by Industry[b]			
Primary	3%	8%	2%
Secondary	28%	30%	23%
Tertiary	69%	62%	75%
CPI (annual growth)	2.1%	35.0%	2.8%
U.S. Exchange Rate	1.37	6.37	1.00
Global Exports of Goods and Services (as % of GDP)	41.8%	26.9%	11.5%
Global Imports of Goods and Services (as % of GDP)	41.6%	14.8%	13.1%
Current Account Balance	–$8.2	–$0.65	–$105.1
Merchandise Trade Balance (billions U.S.$)	$20.7	$7.1	–$173.5
Population (millions)	30	91	263
% of North America	8%	24%	68%
Median Age (years)	34	22	34
Labor Force (millions)	15	34	132
% of North America	8%	19%	73%
Employment (millions)	13.5	32.7	124.9
% of North America	8%	19%	73%
Unemployment Rate	9.5%	4.8%	5.6%
Public and Private Education Spending (as % of GDP)[c]	8.0%	6.2%	7.5%
Adult Population (25–64 years) with Completed College or University Education in 1992[d]	41%	24%	31%

[a] At purchasing power parity.

[b] Primary includes agriculture, forestry, and fishing; secondary includes manufacturing, mining, and construction; and tertiary includes transportation, communications, utilities, community, business and personal services, wholesale and retail trade and finance, insurance and real estate, and government services. Data are 1994 for the United States.

[c] Data are 1994 for the United States.

[d] Data are 1994 for Mexico for the adult population with some college or university education.

Source: Canada, Statistics Canada; Mexico, INEGI and STPS; United States, Department of Labor and Department of Commerce.

of the working population shifted from 10 percent to 8 percent in the primary sector, from 20 percent to 17 percent in manufacturing, and from 70 percent to 75 percent in services during 1984–1995.

A significant development of major concern internationally is the widespread growth in unemployment. In 1995, unemployment in OECD countries amounted to 34.5 million people, or 7.6 percent of the labor force—3.0 million more than in 1983. In contrast, the overall unemployment level in North America dropped from 11.0 million workers in 1984 to 10.5 million workers in 1995, and the unemployment rate decreased from 7.4 percent to 5.8 percent during that period. This drop was mainly due to a lower unemployment rate in the United States, partially offset by increased unemployment in Canada during 1984–1995 and increased unemployment in Mexico in the 1990s.

This profile compares the labor markets of two developed countries with that of a developing country. Such a comparison has inherent difficulties, including the fact that the differences among the countries cannot be measured only in quantitative terms. Concepts such as employment growth, unemployment, underemployment, and nonstandard employment have different meanings. This report explains the different meanings of these concepts in each country when discussed in the text.

For further clarification, the key features of each country's economic and social environment are described below. In addition, this chapter compares the main macroeconomic, demographic, and labor force characteristics of the three countries during 1984–1995 as a backdrop for the remainder of the report.

Canada

Canada is the largest North American country from a geographic standpoint, yet it has the smallest total population and the smallest labor force. The Canadian economy is the most export-oriented of the three NAFTA countries.

Canada's economy is larger than Mexico's but less than 10 percent of the size of the U.S. economy.

During 1984–1989, Canada experienced average annual growth in real GDP of 4.3 percent. This growth was stronger than that of both the United States and Mexico over the same period. Since the 1990–1991 economic recession, however, Canada's real growth has been slower, averaging 2.9 percent annually between 1992 and 1995. This figure was below growth levels of 3.1 percent in the United States. The average inflation rate during 1984–1995 was moderate at 3.8 percent; the average inflation rate during 1992–1995 was very low at 1.4 percent. The service sector has continued to dominate economic growth during the past decade, and economic growth in the primary and manufacturing sectors has slowed. Economic growth in the manufacturing and mining sectors has been stronger since 1992 compared with 1984–1992.

Export growth during 1988–1995 was robust. Worldwide exports of goods and services, as measured by their value in U.S. dollars, grew 61 percent between 1988 and 1995. Imports grew more slowly than exports—at 49 percent during the same period—resulting in a current trade surplus. The United States is Canada's largest trading partner; trade between Canada and Mexico is modest.

Canada had a very high federal debt of $545.7 billion in Canadian dollars during 1994–1995, or 73 percent of GDP. Interest on this debt accounted for 35 percent of total federal government expenditures in 1994–1995. Provincial governments have high levels of debt as well. The government introduced several budget-cutting measures in the past few years to reduce budget deficits. These measures included cuts to the Unemployment Insurance Program and large-scale government downsizing. As a consequence, Canada is projected to have the lowest deficit (1.3 percent) relative to its GDP among G-7 countries in 1996.

Population growth was slower in Canada than in Mexico, growing at a moderate pace of about 1.4 percent annually. However, the country's population is growing more rapidly than any other Western industrialized nation, including the

DATA ISSUES:
Macroeconomics, Demographics, and Labor Force

Chapter I uses data primarily from the following sources:

Source	Agency
Macroeconomic information	
Canadian National Income and Expenditure Accounts	Statistics Canada
Mexican System of National Accounts	National Institute for Statistics, Geography, and Informatics (INEGI)
U.S. National Income and Product Accounts	U.S. Bureau of Economic Analysis
Demographic data	
Canadian Census of the population	Statistics Canada
Mexican General Census of Households and Population	INEGI
U.S. Census of the population	U.S. Bureau of the Census
Labor force data	
Canadian Labor Force Survey (LFS)	Statistics Canada
U.S. Current Population Survey (CPS)	Bureau of Labor Statistics
Mexican National Expenditure and Income Survey (ENIGH)	INEGI
National Employment Survey (ENE)	INEGI and the Ministry of Labor and Social Welfare (STPS)

Data for Canada and Mexico are for workers age 15 and older, while data for the United States are for workers age 16 and older.

The U.S. Current Population Survey was redesigned in 1994. In that same year, population controls based on the 1990 Census were introduced, resulting in a major break in the data series. These changes led to an increase in the number of people reporting some labor force activity. Data for 1994 and 1995 are, therefore, not strictly comparable with earlier years.

In the case of Mexico, data for 1984 are from the ENIGH and data for 1991, 1993, and 1995 are based on the ENE. Mexican labor force data for nonsurvey years for the entire country were interpolated using the survey year data. A description of the differences between the ENIGH and the ENE is provided in the box on pages 28–29.

United States. In the 1990s, Canada's rapid population growth was a result of relatively high net migration levels (which accounted for 59 percent of population growth in 1994). Immigration from North and Central America accounted for only 4 percent of immigration to Canada; most of Canada's immigrants come from Europe and Asia.

The Canadian population is young compared with that of other industrialized countries. However, the population and labor force are aging, and labor force growth is slowing as more of the baby boom generation moves into the 40–50 age bracket. The fastest-growing segments of the population are between the ages of 25 and 54 and over the age of 65.

Among G-7 countries, Canada has the highest percentage of adults with some post-secondary education. It also boasts the second highest level of public spending on education in the OECD after Germany. The education levels of Canadians 15 years old and over have risen significantly in 1984–1994. Slightly more than 13.0 percent of Canadians had less than a high school education in 1994, down from 19.9 percent in 1984. Those with a post-secondary or university education increased from 30.2 percent to 46.5 percent over the decade.

Canada has a tradition of extensive social programs. They include the federal Employment Insurance Program, the federal Canada Pension Plan, and the provincially run Quebec Pension Plan, all of which are funded by employer and employee payroll taxes; the provincial worker's compensation programs, which are supported by an employer payroll tax; and the universal federal Old Age Security, the provincially administered social assistance for the poor, and a national health care system, which are supported through general revenues. Progressive income taxes and transfer payments to unemployed and disadvantaged individuals, as well as substantial public spending on health care and education, have to some extent offset inequality in the distribution of earnings emerging from the labor market. Social programs are currently being reformed in Canada as a result of the country's high debt level and weak labor

market conditions, including persistently high levels of unemployment.

Mexico

Mexico's economy and social structure exhibit certain traits that distinguish it from Canada and the United States. These traits include a lower GDP per capita, a younger population, a rapid labor force growth, a lower rate of female labor force participation, a lower average of earnings, a larger informal sector, and a large proportion of employment in the primary sector. The primary sector accounted for 23.5 percent of total employment and a significantly higher proportion of GDP than in Canada and the United States in 1995.

During 1984–1995, the Mexican economy grew at a real average annual rate of 2.0 percent; however, it fluctuated significantly each year. During 1984–1985, the economy was recovering from the 1982 debt crisis and grew at a real annual rate of 3.1 percent. In 1986, a substantial reduction in international oil prices adversely affected the economy. In 1987, GDP growth dropped to 1 percent and the inflation rate rose to a peak of 159 percent.

Between 1989 and 1994, Mexico implemented eight Pacts for Stabilization and Economic Growth involving business, labor, and government participation. The main objectives of these pacts were to reduce inflation and improve public finances. Wages and salaries were adjusted based on the expected rate of inflation. The economy recovered, and the rate of growth in real GDP increased to 2.6 percent per annum; total investment, both public and private, increased at annual rates of 7.7 percent; the rate of inflation dropped to single-digit levels in 1994; and real wages began to increase.

In 1995, the Mexican economy faced a new crisis with the following: a 50.0 percent drop in the value of the peso against the U.S. dollar, a 6.9 percent drop in GDP, a reduction in the rate of investment of 30.0 percent over 1994, and an annual increase in the consumer price index of 35.0 percent. The scale of the crisis resulted in an increase in the unemployment rate to levels above the 1986 crisis levels and a significant decline in real earnings of 15 percent compared with 1994.

An important shift in Mexican trade policy was made during the past decade with a move toward more open trade. This shift and the economic recovery after 1988 resulted in high annual growth in imports of goods and services (15.9 percent) as well as exports (11.0 percent) between 1988 and 1994. These changes had a tremendous impact on the current account deficit, which increased from U.S.$2.4 billion in 1988 to U.S.$29.4 billion in 1994. In 1995, partly as a result of the sharp devaluation of the peso, exports of goods and services increased by 30.6 percent and imports decreased by 9.1 percent, causing a significant reduction in the current trade deficit. Mexican trade with the United States and Canada experienced substantial growth. By 1995, these countries accounted for 81 percent of Mexico's world trade. Although Mexico's trade with Canada has increased, it remains limited.

A significant factor that influenced Mexico's labor market behavior is rapid population growth. Over the past 40 years, the Mexican population has more than tripled, growing at an average annual rate of 2.9 percent. In the past decade, this rate of growth has slowed considerably to 2 percent annually, mainly because of a significant decline in fertility rates. Rapid growth in the working-age population, combined with the increasing labor force participation of both men and women, contributed to strong labor force growth. Between 1984 and 1995, almost 1 million people entered the labor force annually. The economic crises of the past decade made it difficult to create enough productive jobs to absorb the growing labor force. Many of the new entrants had to join the informal sector. In 1988, the informal sector was estimated to account for 38 percent of total employment.[4]

Although there has been a considerable slowdown in population growth in the 1980s and 1990s, the proportion of the population under 14 years of age remains high (36 percent by 1995). As a consequence, there will be a continued rapid increase in the working-age population over the

next decade. This factor, and continued growth in female labor force participation, will exert a great deal of pressure on the labor market. According to Mexico's National Population Council (CONAPO), the Mexican labor force will increase from 36.4 million to 46.4 million people between 1996 and 2005.

Improved accessibility to a basic education has led to higher levels of schooling for the population in general and workers in particular. The labor force aged 12 years and over increased its average level of schooling from 4.6 years in 1984 to 5.6 years in 1993. Despite this improvement, in 1993 more than half of the Mexican labor force had 6.0 years or less of schooling.

Mexico has maintained a national social security system encompassing retirement income, disability income, health insurance, housing benefits, child care, and other programs. Funding and eligibility for these programs is largely tied to payroll taxes and employment in the formal sector of the economy. In 1995, 44 million people, or 48 percent of the population, were covered by the two major social security institutions: the Mexican Institute for Social Security (IMSS) and the Institute for Security and Social Services for Public Servants (ISSSTE). The IMSS law was reviewed in 1995 and reforms will go into effect in 1997.[5] The country does not have an unemployment insurance system, although it does have a mandatory severance pay system.

United States

The United States has the world's largest, most service-oriented economy. About 7 out of 10 workers in North America live in the United States. During 1984–1989, the United States experienced a real average annual growth of 3.3 percent in GDP. Since the recession of 1990–1991, the rate of economic growth has been slower, averaging 3.1 percent annually between 1992 and 1995, as in Canada. Inflation in 1984–1995 was moderate, averaging 3.9 percent annually. The level of economic growth in the United States has slowed since the 1960s as a result of lower growth

A significant factor that influenced Mexico's labor market behavior is rapid population growth.

Trade accounts for a smaller percentage of GDP in the United States than in Canada and Mexico.

in domestic demand and slower labor productivity growth. Many analysts believe that increased global trade should help boost productivity growth in the future by allowing the country to shift resources to more productive uses.

Trade accounts for a smaller percentage of GDP in the United States than in Canada and Mexico because the size of the U.S. economy allows it to fill more of its own needs. However, U.S. merchandise trade represents a large share of world trade, accounting for 13 percent of world exports and 15 percent of world imports in 1993. Growth in U.S. worldwide trade in goods and services was strong in 1988–1995. Exports grew 83 percent and imports grew by 64 percent, narrowing the trade deficit. Canada is by far the largest trading partner of the United States, followed by Japan and Mexico.

The United States has the lowest rate of population growth in North America. Despite immigration, U.S. population growth averaged only 0.9 percent annually between 1984 and 1995. Nearly 60 percent of U.S. immigrants come from the Western hemisphere, unlike Canada where most immigration is from Asia and Europe. The United States has a fairly young population compared with other industrialized countries. As in Canada, the most rapidly growing segment of the population consists of the 25–54 age group.

The education levels of U.S. workers aged 25 years and over improved substantially in 1985–1992. The number of Americans with less than a high school education shrank from 8.3 percent to 6.0 percent of the population during this period, while the percentage of those with a post-secondary or university education grew from 21.5 percent to 27.3 percent.

The United States has extensive federal and state social programs. The principal federal programs include retirement income and death or disability benefits (which are referred to as "Social Security") and health care for those over age 65 ("Medicare"), both of which are funded by payroll taxes on employers and workers; and general assistance for poor citizens with children ("welfare")

and health insurance for the poor ("Medicaid," which is shared with the states), both of which are funded by general tax revenues. The main state-based programs are unemployment insurance and worker's compensation for job-related injuries and illnesses. Both are funded by employer-paid payroll taxes, adjusted by experience ratings. States also maintain general assistance programs for the poor, funded by general revenues. Social programs at all levels of the U.S. government are undergoing reviews and significant modifications. Many programs are being shifted from the federal jurisdiction to state jurisdictions.

Macroeconomic Structure

Real Gross Domestic Product in North America

As shown in Figure 1, the North American economies had moderate growth in real GDP during 1984–1995. The economies of the United States and Canada exhibited similar growth, rising at an average rate of 2.5 percent per year and 2.4 percent per year, respectively, with a dip during the economic recession of 1990–1991. Canada experienced faster economic growth than the United States in 1984–1989, while the U.S. economy grew more rapidly than Canada's economy after 1992. In contrast, during 1984–1994, the Mexican economy grew at 2.0 percent per annum and Mexico's GDP dropped substantially in 1986 (−3.8 percent) and 1995 (−6.9 percent). All three countries' economies grew more slowly in 1984–1995 than in the previous decade.

There are significant differences in the scale of the three economies. The U.S. economy generated 89 percent of the North American GDP in 1995, while Canada and Mexico accounted for 8 percent and 3 percent, respectively.

For Canada and the United States, growth in output was faster than population growth during 1984–1995. Mexico's output grew at the same pace as population until 1994. In 1995, output growth dipped below population growth.

Figure 1

Real Gross Domestic Product in North America 1984–1995

Index 1984 = 100

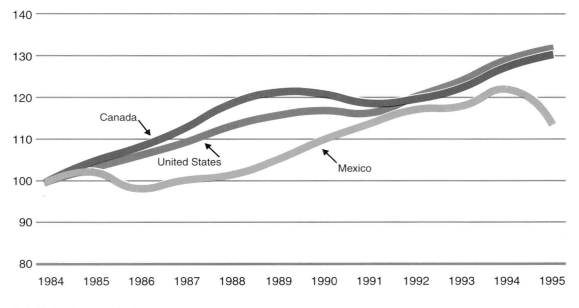

Note: National currency basis.

Source: Canada, Statistics Canada, National Income and Expenditure Accounts; Mexico, INEGI, System of National Accounts; United States, Bureau of Economic Analysis, National Income and Product Accounts.

Total Gross Domestic Investment in North America

As shown in Figure 2, growth in gross domestic investment (GDI) in North American countries fluctuated with the economic cycle during 1984–1995. Before 1990, Canada had the strongest growth in total GDI and the strongest growth in GDP. GDI in Canada as a share of GDP grew from 18.7 percent in 1984 to 23.2 percent in 1989. Between 1989 and 1992, Mexico had the strongest growth in total GDI as a share of GDP, increasing from 17.3 percent to 21.1 percent. While Mexico's economy remained strong during this period, the Canadian and U.S. economies experienced recessions. In 1993 and

1994, the United States had the strongest growth in GDI as a share of GDP. U.S. GDI grew from 18.8 percent in 1993 to almost 20.0 percent of GDP in 1994.

Public and Private Gross Domestic Investment in North America

Fluctuations in public and private investment played a strong role in determining GDI performance. Figure 3 shows the growth rates of public and private investment in the three countries during 1984–1995. In Canada, GDI grew at a rapid rate of 8.4 percent per annum during 1984–1989, contributing to strong economic growth. This rate was mainly due to private investment growth.

Figure 2

Total Gross Domestic Investment in North America
1984–1995

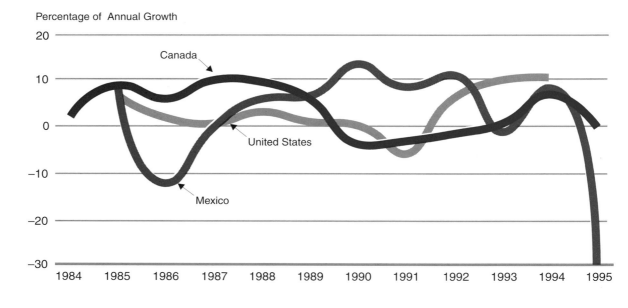

Note: National currency basis.

Source: Canada, Statistics Canada, National Income and Expenditure Accounts; Mexico, INEGI, System of National Accounts; United States, Bureau of Economic Analysis, National Income and Product Accounts.

During the 1990–1991 recession, a sharp decrease in private investment was only partially offset by increased public investment. Private investment remained sluggish until 1994, when it grew by 7.5 percent, only to be followed by a decline of 0.6 percent in 1995.

In the United States, growth in GDI remained fairly flat between 1986 and 1989 and declined during the 1990–1991 recession. This decline was mainly due to a drop in private investment. After 1991, investment growth recovered, rising at an annual rate of 9.5 percent between 1992 and 1994. This recovery contributed to stronger economic growth of over 3 percent in this period.

In Mexico, total GDI growth recovered in 1988 after two years of decline. During 1988–1992, total GDI grew at an average rate of 9.6 percent per annum. This rate was mainly the result of strong private investment growth. The strong growth of GDI fostered increased economic activ-

ity, with GDP growing at 3.5 percent annually. After 1993, however, total GDI declined, and in 1995, it decreased by 30.9 percent, the most pronounced fall in the past 15 years.

Worldwide Exports and Imports of Goods and Services

As shown in Figure 4, total exports and imports of goods and services in U.S. dollars grew throughout North America during 1984–1995. Mexico experienced the fastest growth in imports of goods and services at 10 percent annually. Imports into Canada and the United States grew at similar annual rates—7.5 percent and 7.6 percent, respectively. U.S. exports of goods and services grew at 9.5 percent annually during 1984–1995, compared with 9.0 percent annually in Mexico and 7.3 percent annually in Canada.

On an absolute basis, the United States had the largest trade volume in 1995, with imports and

Figure 3

Public and Private Gross Domestic Investment in North America

Canada, 1984–1995

Percentage of Annual Growth

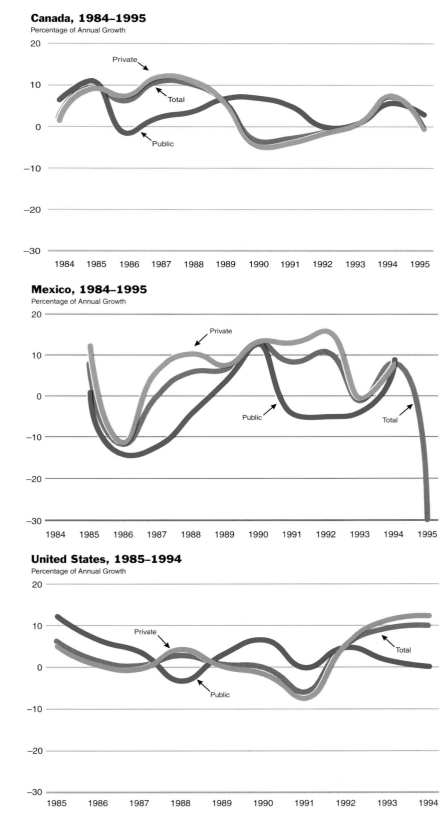

Mexico, 1984–1995

Percentage of Annual Growth

United States, 1985–1994

Percentage of Annual Growth

Note: National currency basis.

Source: Canada, Statistics Canada, National Income and Expenditure Accounts; Mexico, INEGI, System of National Accounts; United States, Bureau of Economic Analysis, National Income and Product Accounts.

Figure 4

Worldwide Exports and Imports of Goods and Services 1984–1995

Canada
Billions in U.S. Dollars

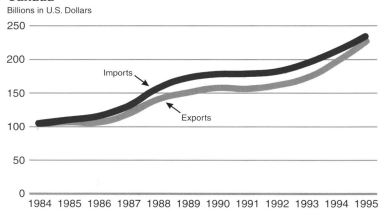

Mexico
Billions in U.S. Dollars

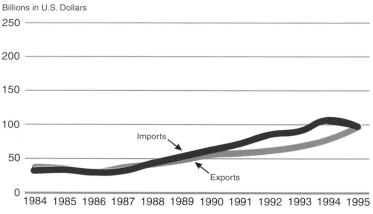

United States
Billions in U.S. Dollars

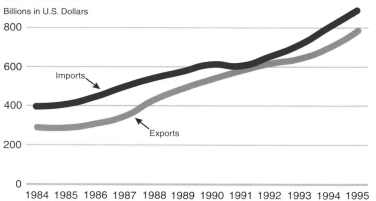

Source: Canada, Statistics Canada, National Income and Expenditure Accounts; Mexico, INEGI, System of National Accounts; United States, Bureau of Economic Analysis, National Income and Product Accounts.

exports of goods and services accounting for U.S.$892.0 billion and U.S.$786.0 billion, respectively. By comparison, Canadian imports and exports accounted for U.S.$236.0 billion and U.S.$227.0 billion in 1995, and Mexican imports and exports accounted for U.S.$98.2 billion and U.S.$97.6 billion in 1995.

North American countries faced sustained deficits in their current account balance of payments during this period. In Canada, notwithstanding the buoyancy in exports, current deficits remained large, reflecting high import propensity and the cost of servicing Canada's large external debt. In 1995, the current account deficit was considerably reduced as a result of a large increase in merchandise exports, which grew 15 percent from the preceding year.

In Mexico, the current account deficit widened between 1989 and 1994. This widening was mainly the result of a sharp increase in the trade deficit as merchandise imports increased at a faster rate (17.9 percent in average per year) than merchandise exports (11.6 percent per annum). In 1995, the current account deficit dropped dramatically as a result of less incoming foreign capital and of a more favorable trade balance. From a deficit of U.S.$18.5 billion in 1994, Mexico's trade balance shifted to a surplus of U.S.$7.1 billion in 1995.

In the United States, the growth in the current account deficit during 1984–1995 was mainly due to a rise in the trade deficit, which increased from U.S.$112.5 billion in 1984 to U.S.$173.5 billion in 1995. The trade deficit grew during that period, despite high growth in merchandise exports (9.1 percent per annum); imports continued growing at a high rate (7.6 percent per year). Unlike Canada and Mexico, the United States showed a service balance surplus throughout 1984–1995.

Worldwide Exports and Imports of Goods and Services as a Percentage of GDP
Figure 5 compares Canada, Mexico, and the United States in terms of worldwide exports and imports of goods and services as a percentage of GDP. It is clear that Canada is more dependent on

Figure 5

Worldwide Exports and Imports of Goods and Services as Percentage of GDP 1984–1995

Exports
Exports as Percentage of GDP

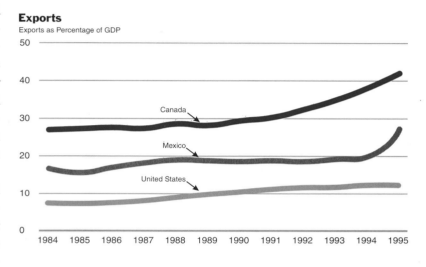

Imports
Imports as Percentage of GDP

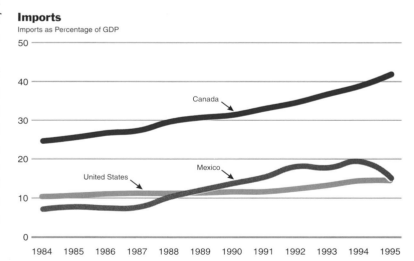

Note: National Account Basis.

Source: Canada, Statistics Canada, National Income and Expenditure Accounts; Mexico, INEGI, System of National Accounts; United States, Bureau of Economic Analysis, National Income and Product Accounts.

Figure 6

Merchandise Exports and Imports in North America
1995

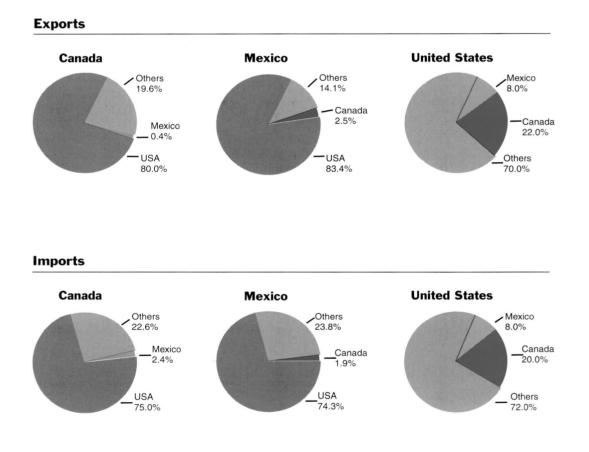

Exports

Canada

Mexico

United States

Imports

Canada

Mexico

United States

Note: National currency basis.

Source: Canada, Statistics Canada; Mexico, INEGI; United States, Bureau of the Census.

trade than are the United States and Mexico. In 1995, Canadian exports of goods and services accounted for 41.8 percent of GDP in real terms; imports accounted for 41.6 percent. Mexican exports and imports accounted for 26.9 and 14.8 percent of GDP, respectively. The United States is the least dependent on trade; exports and imports represented 11.5 and 13.1 percent of GDP, respectively.

As a result of more open trade policies, trade grew as a share of GDP in all three North American countries during 1984–1995. In Mexico, with the adoption of more open trade policies in 1986, imports of goods and services as a proportion of GDP grew from 7 percent in 1986 to 19 percent in 1994, while exports rose from 17 percent to 20 percent of GDP during 1986–1994. The devaluation of the peso at the end of 1994 had a significant impact on trade. Exports increased to almost 27 percent of GDP and imports dropped to 15 percent of GDP in 1995.

For Canada, trade as a share of GDP grew more rapidly in 1988–1995 after the bilateral Free Trade Agreement with the United States. Imports as a proportion of GDP grew from 28 percent in 1988 to 42 percent in 1995; exports rose from 28 percent to 42 percent during the same period.

In the United States, imports of goods and services as a share of GDP rose from 11.0 percent to 13.0 percent and exports increased from 9 percent to 11.5 percent of GDP during 1988–1995.

Merchandise Exports and Imports in North America
Both Canadian and Mexican trade depend heavily on the U.S. market, as can be seen in Figure 6. In 1995, Mexican exports of goods to the United States accounted for 83.4 percent of total exports, while imports of goods from the United States represented 74.3 percent of total imports. In the same year, Canadian exports to the United States accounted for 80 percent of the total, and imports represented 75 percent. U.S. merchandise trade depends less on its NAFTA partners; only 30 percent of exports and 27 percent of imports were within North America in 1995. Nevertheless,

Canada and Mexico remained the first and third largest markets for U.S. trade.

Canada's merchandise trade with the United States sustained a surplus throughout 1984–1995. In 1994 and 1995, the trade surplus grew more rapidly because of increased Canadian exports to the United States. In contrast, Canada had a growing trade deficit with Mexico during 1984–1995 because of increased imports.

Mexico's merchandise trade balance with the United States, its dominant trading partner, shifted from a 1985–1990 surplus to a deficit in 1991–1994. In 1994, U.S. exports to Mexico increased 18 percent and Mexican exports to the United States increased 28 percent, but the devaluation of the Mexican peso in December 1994 caused a 2 percent drop in U.S. exports to Mexico in 1995. As a result, Mexico had a surplus trade balance with the United States of U.S.$12.4 billion in 1995. Canada is Mexico's third largest trading partner. Merchandise trade with Canada increased 18 percent per annum during 1985–1995.

The trade balance of U.S. merchandise with its NAFTA partners was in continuous deficits during 1988–1995. The U.S. trade deficit with Mexico was particularly high in 1995 as a result of the combined effect of a 28 percent increase in imports from Mexico and a 2 percent reduction in exports to Mexico. The U.S. trade deficit with Canada arose mainly because of a substantial increase in Canadian exports to the United States—13.2 percent in 1995.

Demographic Structure

Total Population Growth in North America
Figure 7 shows how the populations of Canada, Mexico, and the United States have grown in the final five decades of the 20th century. From 1950 to 1970, the Mexican population grew rapidly, while population growth rates in Canada and the United States slowed. The rate of population growth in Mexico slowed from 3.3 percent annually between 1970 and 1980 to 1.9 percent annually between 1980 and 1990. Mexico's growth rate

Canada's population grew faster during 1984–1995 than that of any other Western industrialized nation.

Figure 7

Total Population Growth in North America
1950–2000

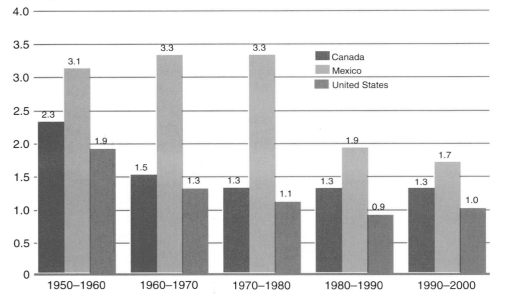

Percentage of Annual Growth

Note: Data for 1990–2000 are projections.

Source: Canada, Statistics Canada, Census; Mexico, INEGI, General Census of Households and Population; United States, Census Bureau, Census.

Figure 8

Labor Force Growth in North America
1985–1995

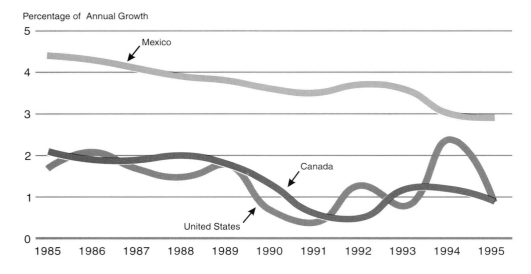

Percentage of Annual Growth

Note: The jump in labor force growth in the United States for 1994 was affected by changes to the Current Population Survey. For Canada and Mexico, figures include workers 15 years and older. For the United States, figures include workers 16 years and older.

Source: Canada, Statistics Canada, Labour Force Survey; Mexico, INEGI, National Income and Expenditure Survey, 1984, and STPS/INEGI National Employment Survey with estimated data for nonsurvey years; United States, Bureau of Labor Statistics, Current Population Survey.

remains above its NAFTA partners, mainly because of higher birth rates.

Canada's population grew faster during 1984–1995—1.4 percent annually faster than that of any other Western industrialized nation, including the United States.

The population of the United States constituted 68.3 percent of the North American population in 1995, or 263 million people. Mexico claimed the next largest population (23.9 percent, or 91 million people), followed by Canada (7.8 percent, or 30 million people).

The age profiles of the populations of the United States and Canada are very similar. In both countries, the highest proportion of the population is concentrated between 24 and 54 years of age. The Mexican population is significantly younger. About 45.0 percent of people in Mexico are under 19 years of age, compared to 28.6 percent and 27.1 percent, respectively, in the United States and Canada.

Labor Force Structure

Labor Force Growth in North America
Figure 8 compares the annual growth of the labor forces of the three North American countries during 1985–1995. The total North American labor force grew rapidly at an average rate of 1.9 percent annually between 1985 and 1995, significantly faster than the labor force growth in European OECD countries (0.7 percent between 1983 and 1993).

In the next decade, most labor force growth in North America will occur in Mexico, where the labor force grew at 3.8 percent annually between 1984 and 1995 compared with 1.4 percent annually in both Canada and the United States. During 1984–1995, the Mexican labor force increased in size by 48 percent or 11 million workers, compared with 17 percent, or 19 million workers, in the United States and 16 percent, or 2 million workers,

in Canada. The labor force increased in Mexico both because its population increased greatly between 1950 and 1970 and because more women began to work. In the United States and Canada, the increased number of women entering the work force was the main cause of growth.

The labor force in North America reached 181 million people in 1995, up from 149 million workers in 1984. North America's share of the labor force of OECD countries was 37 percent in 1995. The United States represented 73 percent of the total North American labor force in 1995, or 132 million workers. In the same year, Mexico accounted for 19 percent, or 34 million workers, and Canada represented 8 percent, or 15 million workers.

The Mexican labor force will continue to grow more rapidly than the labor forces of the United States and Canada. The Mexican labor force is projected to grow by 33 percent, or 11.2 million workers, between 1996 and 2005—mainly because of growth in the working-age population and the increased participation of women. The Canadian labor force is projected to grow by 23 percent, or 3.3 million workers, and the U.S. labor force is projected to grow by 19 percent, or 23.8 million workers, during 1992–2005 because of immigration and the increased participation of women.

Labor Force Participation Rate by Gender
Labor force participation in North America is greater than in European OECD countries—74.9 percent compared with 66.8 percent in 1995 for workers between the ages of 15 and 65.[6] Figure 9 shows that in 1995 the labor force participation of the working-age population (15 or 16 years and older) in Canada and the United States was very similar (65 percent and 67 percent, respectively), while in Mexico participation levels were lower (60 percent). This contrast was mainly due to the significantly lower participation of women in the Mexican labor force. However, during 1984–1995, the Mexican labor force participation rate grew rapidly compared with its North American part-

ners, and it will continue to narrow the gap over the next few years.

The labor force participation of women increased significantly in all three countries during 1984–1995, with Mexico showing the fastest rate of increase. Nevertheless, as Figure 9 shows, female labor force participation in 1995 in Mexico (37 percent) remained substantially lower than rates in the United States (59 percent) and Canada (58 percent). In 1995, women made up 46 percent of the U.S. labor force, 45 percent of the Canadian labor force, and 32 percent of the Mexican labor force.

Change in Labor Force Participation Rate by Gender
Mexico had a higher male labor force participation rate in 1995 than Canada and the United States because there are fewer women in Mexico's labor force and most men, including those over the age of 65 years, need to work in order to maintain sufficient income.

Figure 10 shows the changes among men and women in the labor force during 1984–1995. The labor force participation of Mexican men increased, while the participation of men in the United States and Canada dropped because of early retirement. The participation rate of men dropped more dramatically in Canada than in the United States following the recession in 1990–1991. Between 1990 and 1995, the participation rate of Canadian men dropped from 76.3 percent to 72.8 percent, while in the United States it dropped from 76.1 percent to 75.2 percent.

Labor Force Participation Rate by Age in North America
During 1984–1995, the most rapid growth in labor force participation in Canada and the United States occurred in the 45 to 54 age group, reflecting the aging of the baby boom generation and the fact that more women in this age group are likely to be working. In contrast, in Mexico the most rapid growth was in the 55 to 64 age group.

Nevertheless, as shown in Figure 11, peak labor force participation in all three countries in 1995 occurred between the ages of 25 and 44 years. Labor force participation rates in Canada and the United States were similar for adults between the ages of 20 and 54, while rates in Mexico were lower for all age groups with the exception of workers over 55 years of age.

The United States had the highest participation rate for young workers between the ages of 16 and 24 in 1995, with rates increasing slightly during 1984–1995. In contrast, participation rates for young Canadian workers between the ages of 15

Figure 9

Labor Force Participation Rate by Gender in North America 1995

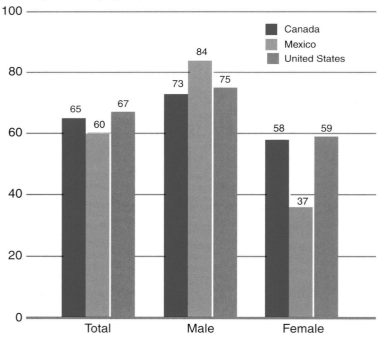

Percentage of Working Age Population

Note: For Canada and Mexico, figures include workers 15 years and older. For the United States, figures include workers 16 years and older.

Source: Canada, Statistics Canada, Labour Force Survey; Mexico, STPS/INEGI, National Employment Survey; United States, Bureau of Labor Statistics, Current Population Survey.

and 24 dropped, particularly during the recession in 1990–1991, because of difficult economic conditions for this age group and rising school enrollment rates. Participation rates for young Mexican workers increased significantly during this period. One of the main reasons for this increase was economic necessity.

Proportionately, Mexico has almost twice as many young people in the labor force compared with the United States and Canada. In 1995, almost 10.0 million Mexican workers, or 29 per-cent of the labor force, were between the ages of 15 and 24. In the same year, 2.5 million, or 17.0 per-cent, of Canadian workers were in this age group and 19.0 million, or 14.3 percent, of U.S. workers were between the ages of 16 and 24.

In 1995, as Figure 11 shows, the United States had the highest labor force participation for the 55 to 64 age group—57 percent. Mexico had 53 per-cent and Canada 48 percent in that year. Participation rates for this age group have risen in the United States as more workers postpone retire-

Figure 10

Change in Labor Force Participation Rate by Gender
1984 and 1995

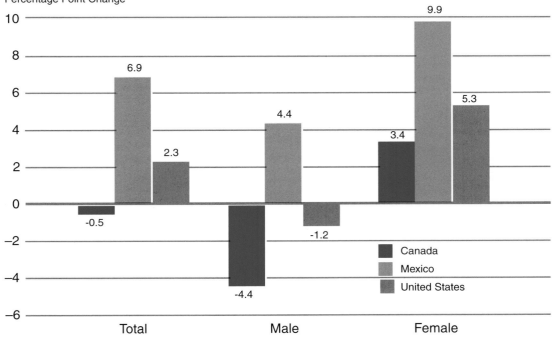

Source: Canada, Statistics Canada, Labour Force Survey; Mexico, INEGI, National Income and Expenditure Survey for 1984 and STPS/INEGI, National Employment Survey, 1995; United States, Bureau of Labor Statistics, Current Population Survey.

Figure 11

Labor Force Participation Rate by Age in North America 1984 and 1995

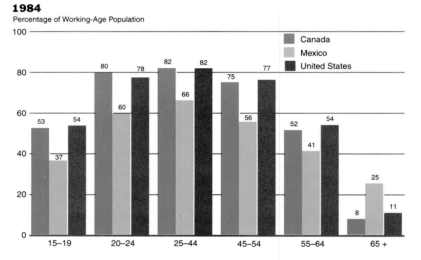

1984
Percentage of Working-Age Population

Legend: Canada, Mexico, United States

1995
Percentage of Working-Age Population

Legend: Canada, Mexico, United States

Note: 1994 for Canada; 16–19 for United States.

Source: Canada, Statistics Canada, Labour Force Survey; Mexico, INEGI, Household Income and Expenditure Survey, 1984, and STPS/INEGI, National Employment Survey, 1995; United States, Bureau of Labor Statistics, Current Population Survey.

ment. The greatest rate increase occurred in Mexico in 1984–1995. In Canada, however, the participation rate of older workers has dropped as a result of fewer job prospects and early retirement. Mexico had the highest labor force participation rates for oldest workers (over the age of 65) in 1995; many of those workers do not have sufficient income to retire. The United States had double Canada's participation rate for oldest workers in 1995, suggesting that more older Americans are remaining in the labor force while their Canadian counterparts retire.

Endnotes

[1] International Monetary Fund, *World Economic Outlook* (Washington, D.C.: International Monetary Fund, October 1996).

[2] OECD, *Employment Outlook* (Paris: Organisation for Economic Co-operation and Development, 1996).

[3] International Labor Organization, *World Employment 1995, An ILO Report* (Geneva: Author, 1995).

[4] For a detailed definition of the informal sector, see page 25.

[5] For a description of the reforms, see page 79.

[6] OECD, *Employment Outlook* (Paris: Organisation for Economic Co-operation and Development, 1996).

CHAPTER II

The Changing Employment Landscape

The Evolution of Employment

Overview

Between 1965 and 1991, the structure of the world's working population shifted from 24 percent to 35 percent in services, from 19 percent to 17 percent in industry, and from 57 percent to 48 percent in the primary sector.[1]

The employment landscape in North America reflects these trends. It is marked by a rapid increase in employment in the service sector; a shift toward managerial, professional, and technical occupations; the growing labor force participation of women; and a significant growth in nonstandard employment. The extent of these changes varies in each country depending on the social and economic context. For example, one of the main labor market characteristics in Mexico is the large proportion of employment in the primary sector. In 1995, this sector absorbed 36 percent of self-employed workers, 60 percent of unpaid workers, and almost 30 percent of part-time workers. Trends in other labor market characteristics are similar for all three countries.

Employment growth in North American countries includes formal and informal employment.

There are different ways of conceptualizing informality. The concept of informality, defined as self-employment, was first used by the International Labor Organization (ILO) in 1972 to analyze employment conditions in Kenya. Since then the concept has changed.[2] Some definitions used in developed countries associate informality with the underground economy.[3] When the United States used this approach, it was estimated that full-time informal employment represented about 4.1 percent of total U.S. employment in 1981.[4] In Canada, the underground economy was estimated to account for less than 2 percent of total employment in 1993.[5] In developing economies, the concept of informality is mainly related to family subsistence criteria. Informality in Mexico, as defined by a combination of class of worker, size of establishment, and industry, was estimated to account for 38 percent of total employment in 1988.[6]

All three countries use internationally recognized standards to measure open unemployment. Open unemployment rates in Mexico have been lower than those in Canada and the United States, but they do not reflect the heterogeneous characteristics of the Mexican labor market. The lack of unemployment insurance and the declining trend in real earnings are two main factors explaining low unemployment rates in Mexico and causing

Service sector employment has increased rapidly in North America.

During

1984–1995,

employment

in the three

countries

increased,

although

annual

growth rates

slowed.

workers to find employment in precarious activities. Thus, in analyzing Mexican employment, one must keep in mind that employment growth covers informal as well as formal employment. To better understand the Mexican labor market, one sees that INEGI has developed nine employment indicators to detect precarious employment conditions. These indicators complement those used for open unemployment. Some of these indicators are discussed in Chapter III.

During 1984–1995, employment in the three countries increased, although annual growth rates slowed. The evolution of employment during this time can be divided into three sub-periods.

Employment Growth (1984–1989)
The three North American countries experienced high employment growth in 1984–1989. Mexico had the highest rate of growth. The level of employment in Mexico increased from 22 million people to 27.5 million, growing at an annual rate of 4.5 percent, while employment in Canada and the United States grew at much lower rates of 2.8 percent and 2.2 percent per annum, respectively. Employment in all three countries grew at higher rates than the labor force, with corresponding declines in unemployment rates.

During this period, employment growth in Mexico occurred in both formal and informal sectors. In spite of low economic growth, the big reduction in real earnings over this period improved the competitiveness of exports and promoted the *maquiladora* industry.[7] During 1984–1989, the number of plants in the *maquiladora* industry more than doubled from 672 to 1,468, helping to sustain employment growth. According to data from the IMSS, from 1984 to 1989 the number of insured employees in the private sector increased at an average annual rate of 6.4 percent.[8] Nevertheless, the formal sector could not create enough jobs to absorb the rapidly increasing labor force. As a result, many workers turned to activities in the informal sector. Household surveys reported an increasing proportion of unpaid family workers during this period,[9] and self-employed workers

accounted for a large proportion of employment (27.7 percent in 1988).

Employment in Canada and the United States also increased in 1984–1989, with higher rates in Canada than in the United States. In both countries, the main factor explaining employment growth was recovery from earlier recessions. The recovery in Canada resulted in average employment growth of 402,000 people per year. In the United States, the average was 2.8 million per year. Canada's real GDP increased at an average annual rate of 3.9 percent, while the U.S. economy rose at 3.1 percent. In Canada, the economic recovery was based on very strong growth in exports and was influenced by the U.S. economic recovery. Economic growth in the United States was mainly due to the recovery in personal consumption and an increase in exports of goods and services.

Employment Contraction (1990–1992)
During the recession of 1990–1992, Canadian employment declined. In the United States, because of the recession of 1990–1991, employment reduced its rate of growth. Labor force growth slowed in both countries. Unemployment rates, which in the preceding six years had declined, rose significantly, reaching their highest levels in 1992 in both countries: 11.3 percent in Canada and 7.4 percent in the United States. In Canada, employment dropped by 81,300 per year, while U.S. employment growth slowed to an average of 85,000 people per year. The main factor explaining this situation was the considerable economic contraction of both economies. Canada's real GDP during 1990–1992 decreased at an average of 0.5 percent per annum, while the U.S. economy reduced its growth to 0.8 percent per annum, well below the levels of the previous period.

In Mexico, employment growth rates were also reduced, but in contrast to Canada and the United States, they continued growing by approximately 3.6 percent annually. As a result, the unemployment rate remained at low levels. The number of insured workers under IMSS rose from 8.0 million workers in 1990 to 8.7 million in 1992, or 4.3

percent. This situation can be explained by two factors. First, the Mexican economy recovered its growth, growing at an annual average rate of 3.2 percent, compared with an average of 1.0 percent in 1984–1989. Second, real earnings began to recover (3.2 percent annual growth), mainly because of a significant reduction in the rate of inflation. The improvement in real earnings influenced the recovery of private consumption, encouraging GDP growth. Nevertheless, the 1991 National Employment Survey indicated that 24 percent of workers were self-employed, and 11 percent were unpaid, suggesting that employment in the informal sector remained high.

Employment Recovery in Canada and the United States, and Employment Contraction in Mexico (1993–1995)
In 1992, Canada and the United States began a period of recovery after two years of stagnation and recession. Employment growth began to increase but at lower rates than in 1984–1989. In both countries, employment grew more quickly than the labor force, resulting in lower unemployment rates. In Canada, employment growth averaged 225,000 per year, while in the United States the average was 2.4 million per year. Some of the changes in U.S. employment figures could be due to modifications to the Current Population Survey in January 1994 (see the box titled Data Issues on pages 28–29 for more details).

In Mexico, real GDP contracted 3.6 percent between 1993 and 1995 and adversely affected employment growth, whose annual rate of growth was reduced from 3.3 percent between 1990 and 1992 to 1.7 percent between 1993 and 1995. Employment in the private formal sector decreased. The average number of permanent workers covered by the IMSS dropped from 8.7 million in 1993 to 8.5 million in 1995. Unemployment increased substantially. In 1995, total unemployment was estimated at 1.7 million, or 4.8 percent of the total labor force. This was the highest unemployment rate in 1984–1995. In the manufacturing sector, employment growth slowed, while employment in retail trade and in personal services grew at high rates of 5.8 percent and 5.6 percent, respectively. This change suggests an increase in informal employment, because a large proportion of self-employed and unpaid workers are engaged in these activities. In-bond industries, or *maquiladoras*, were the main source of manufacturing employment. During 1993–1995, employment in *maquiladoras* grew at 18.7 percent. In 1995, *maquiladoras* accounted for 644,000 workers, or almost 8 percent of employees covered by social insurance through the IMSS.

Employment Growth

Index of Employment Growth in North America
As shown in Figure 12, employment in North America rose from 138.3 million workers in 1984 to 171.1 million in 1995, or an average rate of 2

Figure 12

Index of Employment Growth in North America 1984–1995

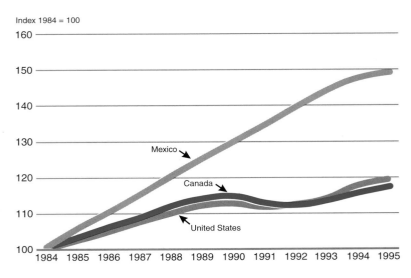

Note: For Canada and Mexico, figures include workers 15 years and older; for the United States, figures include workers 16 years and older.

Source: Canada, Statistics Canada, Labour Force Survey; Mexico, INEGI, National Income and Expenditure Survey, 1984, and STPS/INEGI, National Employment Survey, 1991, 1993, and 1995, with estimated data for non-survey years; United States, Bureau of Labor Statistics, Current Population Survey.

DATA ISSUES:

Employment

Sources of Information

This section uses data primarily from the following household surveys:

Source	Agency
LFS, monthly	Statistics Canada
U.S. Current Population Survey, monthly	U.S. Bureau of Labor Statistics
ENE	INEGI and STPS
ENIGH	INEGI

The ENE Survey began in 1988 and was conducted again in 1991, 1993, and 1995. Data from the ENIGH, carried out periodically by the INEGI, are also used.

The U.S. Current Population Survey has been expanded and modified several times since it began in 1940. In 1994, it underwent a major redesign intended primarily to improve the quality of labor market information. That same year, population controls were introduced based on the 1990 Census, resulting in a major break in the data series. Thus, U.S. data for 1994 and 1995 are not strictly comparable with earlier years. The most relevant results of these changes affecting employment growth were an increase in the number of people reporting some labor force activity and an increase in the unemployment rate.[a] The estimated and adjusted effect of the introduction of the population controls was to raise 1990 employment by 879,000 and raise the overall unemployment rate by 0.1 percentage point.

The LFS began in 1945 at quarterly intervals. Since 1952, it has been carried out monthly. LFS estimates have been revised historically to 1976 to incorporate a new population base using the results of the 1991 Census. There were no significant changes in the LFS during 1984–1995. In 1995, the definition of part-time workers was changed to include hours of work in the main job rather than hours in all jobs. However, for this study, the definition that includes all jobs was used to ensure comparability with U.S. data.

In the case of Mexico, the analysis is based on data from the ENE in 1991, 1993, and 1995. Because of problems in the ENE's 1988 sampling scheme, the results of that year's survey were not used. To cover 1984, the analysis used data from the ENIGH. Data from social security registers at the IMSS were used to complement total employment data and to evaluate employment trends in the private formal sector. Employment data for nonsurvey years were estimated from the difference between labor force and unemployment estimations. (See the discussions on pages 9 and 68–69 in Chapters I and III.)

The ENE and ENIGH Surveys are not completely comparable.[b] The ENIGH was not designed to measure employment, and it does not add questions to capture marginal workers as the ENE does. Thus, the number of self-employed and unpaid family workers might be underestimated. Notwithstanding these differences, information from the ENIGH was considered useful for the analysis because labor force data are consistent with other sources of information, such as the Continuous Occupational Survey of 1979 and the ENE Surveys.[c] However, the reader should be aware that the results presented in this study are affected by differences in these two sources of information.

Some of the main differences between the ENIGH and the ENE are as follows:
- sample size
- reference period—one month for the ENIGH versus one week for the ENE
- time of year that the survey was conducted—the third quarter versus the second quarter
- the definition of employment. The ENIGH classified people who were beginning a job in the next 30 days unemployed; the ENE classified them as employed.

The ENE's concepts and definitions did not change substantially between 1988 and 1995. In 1993, a change in the definition of self-employed and employer categories of workers was made: agricultural workers who employed occasional temporary workers only were moved from the employer category to the self-employed category. To account for this change, STPS prepared special tabulations to make 1991 data comparable with later years. In 1995, the sample size for rural areas was changed from 5,075 households in 1991 to 7,240 households in 1995.

Conceptual Differences

There are certain differences in the three countries' concepts of employment. Mexico and Canada consider unpaid workers who worked at least one hour in the reference period to be employed, while in the United States unpaid workers are required to work at least 15 hours to be considered employed. Another difference is that the Mexican definition considers as employed those people who expect either to start or to return to work within four weeks. In Mexico, people waiting to start a new job accounted for 0.9 percent of total employment in 1995.[d] In Canada and the United States, such workers are considered unemployed.

The U.S., Canadian, and Mexican labor force statistics vary in the lower age limit set for enumeration in the surveys. The United States uses 16 years as the lower age limit of the labor force, Canada uses 15 years, and Mexico uses 12 years. To improve comparability among the countries, the Secretariat of Labor and Social Welfare prepared special tabulations of the Mexican data that would raise the lower limit to 15 years.

For Mexico, employment data refer to the second quarter of the respective year, while for Canada and the United States the data refer to the whole year.

Another important difference is the definition of self-employed workers, wage and salary workers, and employers. In the United States, self-employed persons are those who work for profit or fees in their own business, profession, trade, or farm. Only the unincorporated self-employed are included in the self-employed category. Self-employed persons who respond that their businesses are incorporated are included among wage and salary workers. The term "incorporated" is used for those businesses legally constituted as corporations. In Mexico and Canada, however, the definition of wage and salary workers does not include incorporated self-employed persons.

As a consequence, the number of wage and salary workers in the United States could be overstated when compared with the other countries. Employers in Canada and in Mexico are in a separate category defined as those self-employed persons who have paid employees. In the United States, such employers are included in the self-employed category.

[a] For more detailed information, see "Revisions in Current Population Survey, Effective January 1994," in *Issues in Employment and Earnings*, February 1994.

[b] Mercedes Pedrero, "Estado Actual de las Estadísticas sobre Empleo en México," in *Cuadernos de Trabajo* 4, Secretaría del Trabajo y Previsión Social, Mexico, 1994.

[c] Comparing labor force and employment data from the Continuous Employment Survey 1979, the ENIGH Survey 1984, and the ENE Survey 1991, the following annual growth rates were obtained:

	1979–1991	1984–1991
Labor Force	3.9	4.0
Employment	4.0	4.3

Participation rates of the three surveys were as follows:

1979	(ECSO)	45.5%
1984	(ENIGH)	47.6%
1991	(ENE)	53.6%
1993	(ENE)	55.2%
1995	(ENE)	55.6%

[d] For more detailed information, see Susan Fleck and Constance Sorrentino, "Employment and Unemployment in Mexico's Labor Force," *Monthly Labor Review*, November 1994, U.S. Department of Labor.

Figure 13

Annual Change in Employment in North America 1985–1995

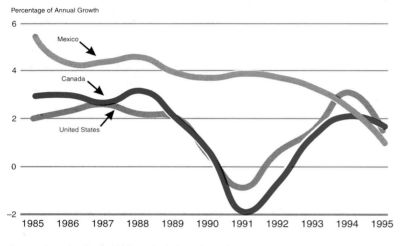

Source: Canada, Statistics Canada, Labour Force Survey; Mexico, INEGI, National Income and Expenditure Survey, 1984, STPS/INEGI, National Employment Survey, 1991, 1993, and 1995, with estimated data for non-survey years; United States, Bureau of Labor Statistics, Current Population Survey.

Figure 14

Absolute Employment Growth in North America 1984–1995

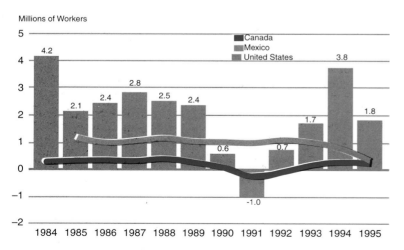

Source: Canada, Statistics Canada, Labour Force Survey; Mexico, INEGI, National Income and Expenditure Survey, 1984, STPS/INEGI, National Employment Survey, 1991, 1993, and 1995, with estimated data for non-survey years; United States, Bureau of Labor Statistics, Current Population Survey.

percent per annum. Thus, over a period of 11 years, employment in North America increased by almost 24 percent. This situation was partly because of the increasing participation of women in the labor force in all three countries, but it also reflects the growth of the working age population.

In 1995, the United States accounted for 73 percent of total employment in North America with 125.0 million workers, followed by Mexico with 19 percent (33.0 million workers) and Canada with 8 percent (13.5 million workers).

Annual Change in Employment in North America
Figure 13, which compares the three countries' total employment growth during 1984–1995, shows that Mexico experienced the highest rate of employment growth. Employment grew at an average annual rate of 3.7 percent, while in the United States and Canada employment grew at much lower rates of 1.6 percent and 1.5 percent, respectively. In Mexico, the increasing share of employment in small firms and in retail trade activities suggests that part of this employment growth occurred in the informal sector.

Although employment levels in the three countries have increased, annual growth rates slowed in 1984–1995, as can be seen in Figure 13. Canada's average annual rate of employment growth slowed from 2.8 percent between 1984 and 1989 to 0.5 percent in 1990–1995. Comparing the same two periods, Mexico's employment growth rate decreased from 4.8 percent to 2.8 percent, while the rate of U.S. employment growth dropped from 2.3 percent to 1.6 percent.

Absolute Employment Growth in North America
Figure 14 shows increases and decreases in growth of employment in North America. The economic recovery in Canada and the United States during 1984–1989 resulted in average employment growth of 402,000 and 2.8 million people per year, respectively. During the recession of 1990 and 1991, Canadian employment declined and U.S. employment reduced its rate of growth. In 1992, Canada and the United States began a period of

recovery and employment growth began to increase. In Canada, employment growth averaged 225,000 per year, while in the United States the average was 2.4 million per year, during 1993–1995. In Mexico, formal and informal employment growth was reduced from an average of 1.1 million per year between 1984 and 1989 to 705,000 per year between 1993 and 1995. The economic crisis in 1995 reduced employment growth to an average of 112,000 people per year.

*Real GDP and Employment Growth
in North America*

In 1984–1995, employment grew in the context of increasing labor productivity (in terms of output per person employed). Figure 15 compares employment growth and GDP for the three North American countries during this period. Canadian and U.S. GDP grew faster than employment, indicating an increase in labor productivity. By contrast, in Mexico formal and informal employment growth occurred in a context of declining output per person employed, with GDP growing at a lower rate than employment. The difference might be explained by the increasing participation of workers in the informal sector in Mexico, where levels of output are lower or where output is not totally accounted for in the national accounts.

In Canada and the United States, the gap between employment and GDP growth widened after 1992, indicating an increase in labor productivity in terms of output per person employed. In Mexico, formal and informal employment continued growing at a higher rate than GDP, reflecting the falling productivity in terms of output per person employed.

*Employment Growth by Gender
in North America*

Employment growth in 1984–1995 was significantly influenced by the increasing participation of women in the labor force in all three countries. Figure 16 shows trends in employment growth for male and female workers in the three North American countries during this period.

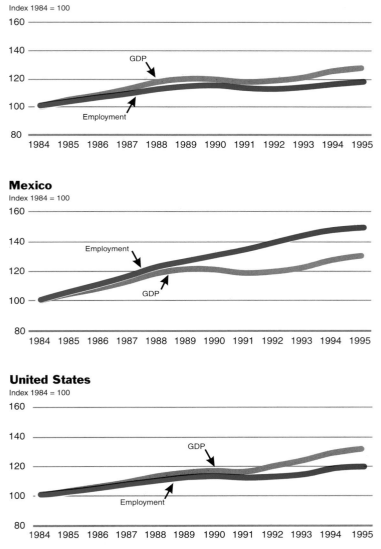

Figure 15

Real GDP and Employment Growth in North America 1984–1995

Canada
Index 1984 = 100

Mexico
Index 1984 = 100

United States
Index 1984 = 100

Note: National currency basis. For the United States, employment growth refers to the first three quarters for 1995.

Source: Canada, Statistics Canada, Labour Force Survey and National Income and Expenditure Accounts. Mexico, INEGI, System of National Accounts; STPS/INEGI, National Employment Survey, 1991, 1993, and 1995; National Income and Expenditure Survey, 1984, with estimated data for non-survey years. United States, Bureau of Economic Analysis, National Income and Product Accounts; Bureau of Labor Statistics, Current Population Survey.

Figure 16

Employment Growth by Gender in North America 1984–1995

Canada
Index 1984 = 100

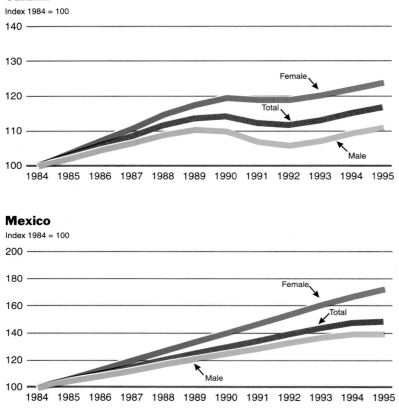

Mexico
Index 1984 = 100

United States
Index 1984 = 100

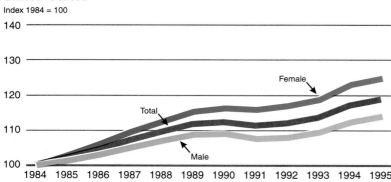

Source: Canada, Statistics Canada, Labour Force Survey; Mexico, INEGI, National Income and Expenditure Survey, 1984, STPS/INEGI, National Employment Survey, 1991, 1993, and 1995, with estimated data for non-survey years; United States, Bureau of Labor Statistics, Current Population Survey.

In Canada, female employment grew 28 percent compared to 12 percent for males. In the United States, female employment rose by almost 25 percent while male employment grew by 14 percent. In Mexico, female employment had the highest increase in North America at 72 percent, while male employment increased by 39 percent. In spite of these changes, the ratio of male to female employment is still 2.1:1 in Mexico and 1.2:1 in Canada and the United States.

Employment by Age and Gender in North America
Female employment in North American countries varies significantly by age. Figure 17 shows that the distribution of female employment is similar in Canada and the United States. Mexico's distribution is distinct, mainly because of the lower share of employed women between 25 and 54 years of age. In contrast, Canadian female workers' employment share in this age group is the highest among North American countries.

Mexico has the highest share of employed men between 15 and 24 years of age and over 55 years of age. The employment share of Canadian men is lower in these groups, particularly among older men.

Employment Structure

Employment by Industrial Sector in North America
Figure 18 shows employment percentages in a number of industries in the three North American countries in 1995. There are important differences in the sectoral distribution of employment in the three countries. One of the major differences is the relatively high level of primary (agriculture, forestry, and fishing) employment in Mexico. Although employment in this sector has substantially declined, it still accounted for almost 24 percent of total employment in 1995. This percentage compares to 4 percent and less than 3 percent in Canada and the United States, respectively. The high employment share of the primary sector in Mexico has a great influence on its labor market characteristics, since this sector absorbs a large proportion of self-employed and unpaid workers.

Figure 17

Employment by Age and Gender in North America
1995

Male
Percentage of Total Employment

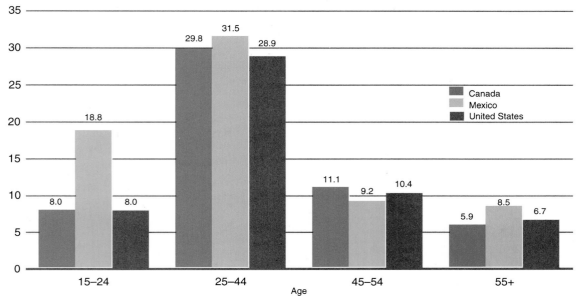

Female
Percentage of Total Employment

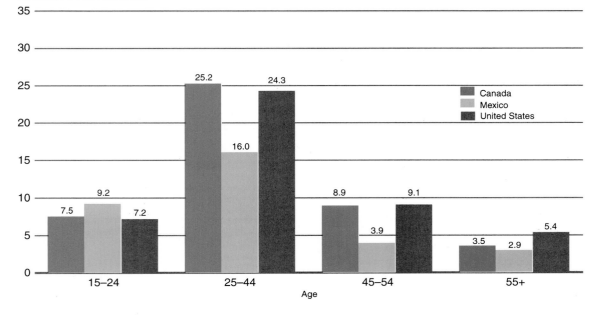

Note: For the United States, figures refer to 16–24 age group.

Source: Canada, Statistics Canada, Labour Force Survey; Mexico, STPS/INEGI, National Employment Survey; United States, Bureau of Labor Statistics, Current Population Survey.

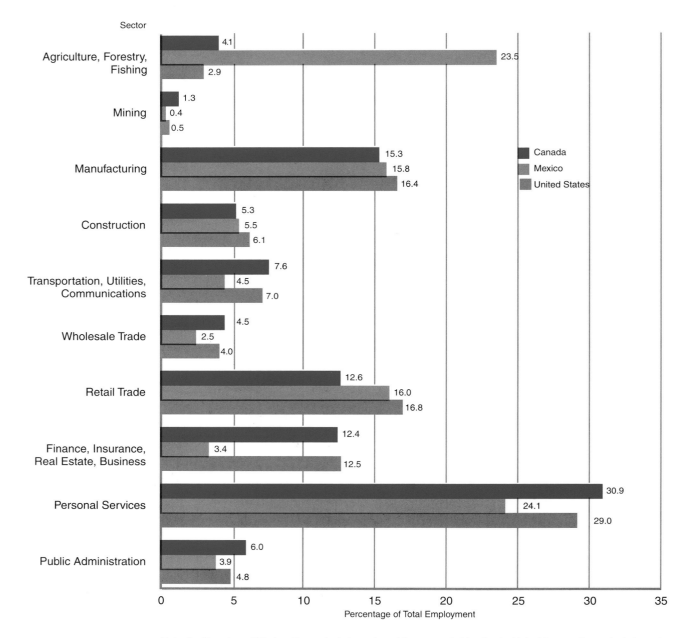

Figure 18

Employment by Industrial Sector in North America
1995

Sector

Agriculture, Forestry, Fishing — Canada 4.1, Mexico 23.5, United States 2.9

Mining — Canada 1.3, Mexico 0.4, United States 0.5

Manufacturing — Canada 15.3, Mexico 15.8, United States 16.4

Construction — Canada 5.3, Mexico 5.5, United States 6.1

Transportation, Utilities, Communications — Canada 7.6, Mexico 4.5, United States 7.0

Wholesale Trade — Canada 4.5, Mexico 2.5, United States 4.0

Retail Trade — Canada 12.6, Mexico 16.0, United States 16.8

Finance, Insurance, Real Estate, Business — Canada 12.4, Mexico 3.4, United States 12.5

Personal Services — Canada 30.9, Mexico 24.1, United States 29.0

Public Administration — Canada 6.0, Mexico 3.9, United States 4.8

Legend: Canada, Mexico, United States

Percentage of Total Employment

Note: For Canada and Mexico, figures include workers 15 years and older; for the United States, figures include workers 16 years and older. Data for Mexico may not equal 100 because of non-specified survey responses.

Source: Canada, Statistics Canada, Labour Force Survey; Mexico, STPS/INEGI, National Employment Survey; United States, Bureau of Labor Statistics, Current Population Survey.

In 1995, those workers accounted for 68 percent of total employment in the primary sector.

Another difference was that in Canada and the United States, employment in the service sector (including transportation, utilities, communications, trade, financial business, personal services, and public administration) was higher (around 74 percent of total employment for both countries in 1995) than in Mexico (54.4 percent in the same year).

Figure 18 also highlights some structural differences among the three countries within the service sector. While all three countries had a relatively high share of employment in personal services in 1995, Mexico also had a higher share of employment in retail trade. Canada had a greater proportion of employment in financial, insurance, real estate, and business services and in public administration. The United States had a greater share of employment in financial, insurance, real estate, and business services and in the retail trade sector.

Change in the Share of Employment by Industrial Sector in North America

The sectoral structure of employment in all three countries changed in 1984–1995. As Figure 19 shows, the main changes were increased employment growth in the service sector, as well as diminished employment in the primary and industry sectors. The service sector was the major source of employment growth. In Canada, 96 percent of employment growth between 1984 and 1995 occurred in the service sector. For the United States, the proportion was 98 percent, while in Mexico, 91 percent of employment growth occurred in the service sector during 1991–1995.

Financial, insurance, real estate, business and personal services were the major areas of Canada's employment growth, while personal services in the United States and retail trade in Mexico represented the chief sources of those countries' employment growth.

Employment by Occupation in North America

The occupational structure of employment in North American countries is directly related to each country's sectoral distribution of employment. Figure 20 gives a snapshot of this distribution in 1995. It shows, for instance, that in Mexico, where a large proportion of workers are in the primary sector, farming accounted for a large share of employment. In Canada and the United States where service sector employment is more prevalent, the main group was managerial, professional, and technical occupations, which accounted for one-third of total employment in 1995.

Another significant group in all three countries is processing occupations, that is, those occupations related to the manufacturing sector. These occupations were the second most important in terms of employment in all three countries. Mexico's employment share of processing occupations in 1995 was much higher (23 percent) than that of Canada or the United States (17 percent). This occupational group experienced the greatest drop in employment in Canada and in the United States during 1984–1995.

Change in Employment by Occupation in North America

Figure 21 shows that increasing employment in the service sector has resulted in more employment in managerial, professional, and technical occupations in Canada and the United States and in more employment in sales occupations in Mexico. The increased employment share of the first three groups, which usually are more skilled positions, was more significant in Canada than in the United States. In contrast, growth in the sales occupations was considerably higher in Mexico than in the United States and Canada. As primary and secondary sectors have reduced their employment share in all three countries, occupations related to these sectors have also reduced their share of total employment.

Increased employment in more skilled positions was more common in the United States and Canada.

Figure 19

Change in the Share of Employment by Industrial Sector in North America 1984–1995

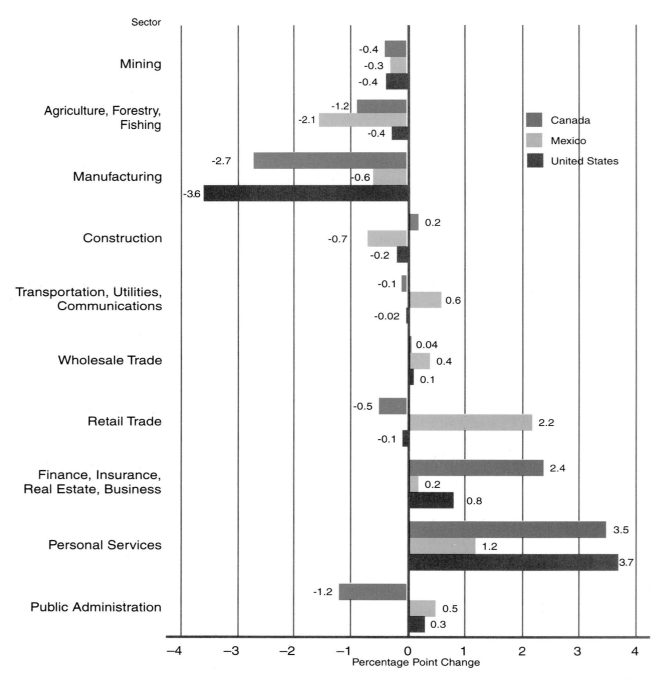

Note: Figures are from 1991 and 1995 for Mexico.

Source: Canada, Statistics Canada, Labour Force Survey; Mexico, STPS/INEGI, National Employment Survey; United States, Bureau of Labor Statistics, Current Population Survey.

Figure 20

Employment by Occupation in North America
1995

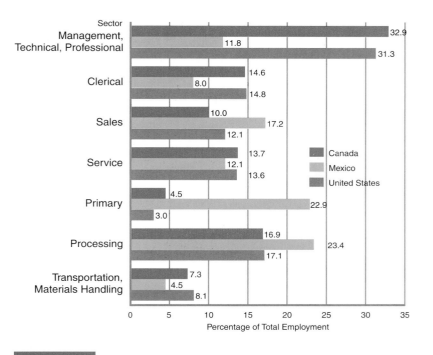

Note: For Canada and Mexico, figures include workers 15 years and older; for the United States, figures include workers 16 years and older. United States data refer to the first three quarters of 1995.

Source: Canada, Statistics Canada, Labour Force Survey; Mexico, STPS/INEGI, National Employment Survey; United States, Bureau of Labor Statistics, Current Population Survey.

Figure 21

Change in the Share of Employment by Occupation in North America
1984 and 1995

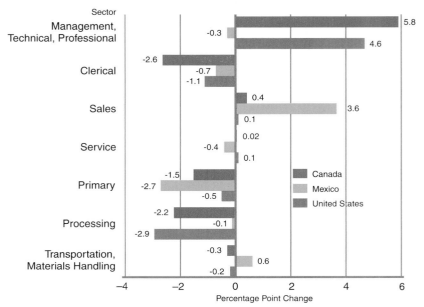

Note: Figures are from 1991 and 1995 for Mexico.

Source: Canada, Statistics Canada, Labour Force Survey; Mexico, STPS/INEGI, National Employment Survey; United States, Bureau of Labor Statistics, Current Population Survey.

Figure 22

Employment by Occupation and Gender in North America
1995

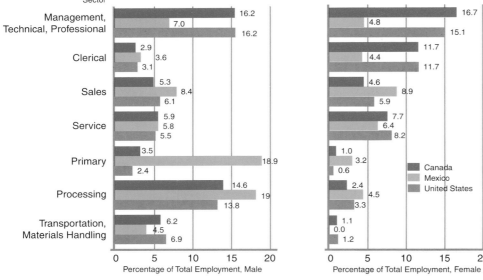

Note: For Canada and Mexico, figures include workers 15 years and older; for the United States, figures include workers 16 years and older.

Source: Canada, Statistics Canada, Labour Force Survey; Mexico, STPS/INEGI, National Employment Survey; United States, Bureau of Labor Statistics, Current Population Survey.

Figure 23

Employment by Class of Worker in North America
1995

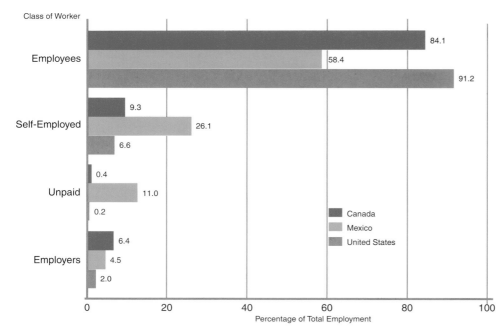

Note: For Canada and Mexico, figures include workers 15 years and older; for the United States, figures include workers 16 years and older.

Source: Canada, Statistics Canada, Labour Force Survey; Mexico, STPS/INEGI, National Employment Survey; United States, Bureau of Labor Statistics, Current Population Survey.

*Employment by Occupation and Gender
in North America*

Figure 22 shows that in all three countries during 1995, clerical and service occupations were occupied mainly by women, while primary, processing, and transportation and materials handling occupations were occupied mainly by men. In Canada and in the United States, managerial, professional, and technical occupations, which accounted for a large share of total employment, were occupied by both men and women in similar proportions. In contrast, these occupations were occupied mainly by men in Mexico.

Employment by Class of Worker in North America

As shown in Figure 23, wage and salary employees are the dominant group of workers in all three countries, particularly in the United States and Canada, where this group represented more than 80 percent of total employment in 1995. In contrast, only 58.4 percent of all workers in Mexico fell into this category.

"Own-account self-employed" workers (i.e., with no employees) are the second most important class of worker in the three countries.[10] In 1995, the share of self-employed and unpaid workers (37.1 percent) in total employment was higher in Mexico than in Canada and the United States (less than 10 percent). This situation was highly influenced by the large employment share of the primary sector in Mexico, where a large proportion of workers fall into this category. Canada had a higher percentage of own-account self-employed workers than did the United States, even when definitional differences were taken into account. In both countries, the share of unpaid workers in total employment was very low (less than 1 percent), while it was significantly higher in Mexico (11 percent).

*Change in the Share of Employment by Class of
Worker in North America*

In 1984–1995, the share of wage and salary employees in total Canadian employment declined, while the share of self-employment

increased as shown in Figure 24. Between 1991 and 1995, the share of employees in total employment in Mexico increased, while the share of self-employed workers decreased. In the United States, there were no major changes in the structure of employment by class of worker during 1984–1995.

Employment by Firm Size in North America

There are important differences in the distribution of employment by firm size among North American countries, as illustrated in Figure 25.

Figure 24

**Change in the Share of Employment by Class of Worker in North America
1984–1995**

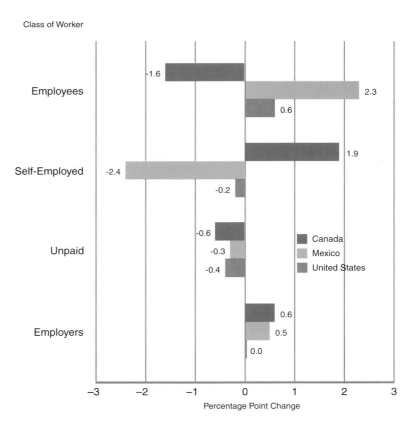

Note: Figures span 1991–1995 for Mexico. For the United States, "Employers" are included in the "Self-Employed" category.

Source: Canada, Statistics Canada, Labour Force Survey; Mexico, STPS/INEGI, National Employment Survey; United States, Bureau of Labor Statistics, Current Population Survey.

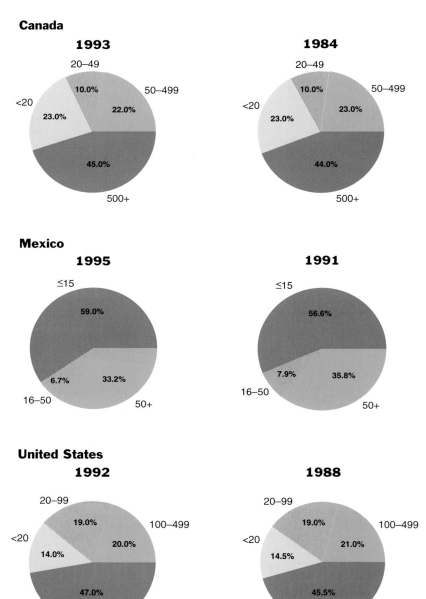

Figure 25

Employment by Firm Size in North America

Canada

1993

20–49
10.0%
<20 50–499
23.0% 22.0%
45.0%
500+

1984

20–49
10.0%
<20 50–499
23.0% 23.0%
44.0%
500+

Mexico

1995

≤15
59.0%
6.7% 33.2%
16–50 50+

1991

≤15
56.6%
7.9% 35.8%
16–50 50+

United States

1992

20–99
19.0%
<20 100–499
14.0% 20.0%
47.0%
500+

1988

20–99
19.0%
<20 100–499
14.5% 21.0%
45.5%
500+

Note: The figures represent number of employees. Firm size is defined according to the number of workers. For Mexico, data exclude workers in agriculture, fishing, trapping, and forestry.

Source: Canada, Statistics Canada, Labour Force Survey; Mexico, STPS/INEGI, National Employment Survey; United States, Bureau of Labor Statistics, Current Population Survey.

Most nonfarm employment in Mexico is in small firms: 59 percent of total nonfarm employment in 1995 was in establishments of 15 workers or fewer. In contrast, Canada had 23 percent and the United States had 20 percent of employment in establishments with fewer than 20 employees in 1993 and 1992, respectively. In Canada and the United States, nearly half the work force was in establishments of more than 500 workers in 1992 and 1993, respectively.

In Mexico, the proportion of employment in small firms (fewer than 15 employees) increased from 57 percent in 1991 to 59 percent in 1995. The share of employment in firms with over 50 employees dropped during the same period. In contrast, Canadian employment by firm size remained virtually unchanged between 1984 and 1993. The United States had a slight increase in the share of employment in firms of more than 500 workers, from 45.5 percent in 1988 to 47.0 percent in 1992.

Working Time and Nonstandard Work

Overview

The largest share of North American workers still hold a single full-time, paid job of indeterminate duration. However, the relative size of this group is declining. Nonstandard employment, including part-time work, own-account self-employment, temporary or contract work, and holding multiple jobs, is becoming more common in all three countries. More workers are combining part-time and temporary paid jobs with jobs they create for themselves. The growth in nonstandard work is reflected in changes in hours of work. Fewer North Americans are working a standard 40- to 48-hour week, and more are working either shorter or longer hours. These trends are affected not only by the economic cycle, but also by deeper structural changes.

Three main forces are driving the growth in nonstandard work and the shifts in working time: technological and organizational change, worker-initiated change, and employer-initiated change.

Technological and Organizational Change

There are several ways in which technological and organizational change have spurred growth in nonstandard work and changes in working hours. The intensive use of nonstandard working arrangements and flexible hours has resulted from technological advances (such as electronic inventory control and scanning); organizational changes involving flexibility and the requirement to develop multiple skills; and greater demand for services in the evenings, on weekends, and in short, peak-service demand periods throughout the service, wholesale, and retail trade sectors.

In the goods-producing sectors, technology-driven "just-in-time" production techniques (where goods are produced just before they are needed by the customer) have encouraged more flexible organizational structures, such as irregular shift work or the formation of a core of full-time workers supplemented by flexible workers with nonstandard arrangements. The flexible employees may work shorter hours or on a temporary basis during peak periods. These flexible organizational structures have increased the demand for various services outside normal working hours, both to accommodate people who work nonstandard hours and to provide services to the goods-producing facility.[11]

Inexpensive computers, modems, fax machines, and cellular telephones have made it possible for more people to become self-employed or to work at home. More intense use of computers can increase both job creation and job destruction, or can cause labor market "churning."[12]

Worker-Initiated Change

The influx of women into the labor force in all three countries and the corresponding growth in two-income families have led many workers to call for more flexible work arrangements, including longer or shorter hours and temporary or part-time work assignments. These voluntary arrangements enable workers to reconcile work responsibilities with other personal interests, such as family responsibilities, education, and leisure. They may provide the opportunity to gain work experience, earn a higher income, improve work diversity, have greater mobility, or learn multiple skills. As noted in the analysis below, most part-time work in North America is voluntary.

Growth in voluntary, own-account self-employment can benefit both workers and the economy by helping the unemployed generate work for themselves, by stimulating the development of small business, and by encouraging entrepreneurs. It also gives workers greater control over hours and working conditions.

These changes have led to increased demand for services outside normal working hours to accommodate working families. Demand for personal services stores, groceries, fast-food, cleaning, and the like has in turn encouraged growth in nonstandard employment in these industries.[13]

Employers can benefit from worker-initiated flexible work arrangements. They may improve their efficiency through greater flexibility in adjusting to changing work force needs. For example, they can cope with irregular business levels by temporarily augmenting or reducing the work force. Greater flexibility can give employers better control of labor costs, the ability to cover for absent employees, higher productivity, and better morale.

When worker-initiated, nonstandard arrangements concerning work place and time are involuntary, they can be a symptom of labor market difficulties, such as inadequate income and benefits, along with job insecurity. Many North American workers in nonstandard arrangements have less access to secure, adequate incomes and they receive inferior benefits. Benefits affected may include pensions, vacations, unemployment insurance, and health coverage. See Chapter IV for an analysis of benefits for nonstandard workers. For example, the growth in multiple job holders may reflect the inability of workers to find one job that pays

Fewer North Americans are working a standard 40- to 48-hour week, and more are working either shorter or longer hours.

enough to meet regular expenses. Many workers in North America receive low hourly rates and need to work overtime to generate sufficient income. High levels of own-account self-employment in Mexico often reflect the insufficient creation of formal jobs and the need to meet immediate income needs. Incomes among the own-account self-employed in North America are significantly lower than in paid employment, and many of these workers are without benefits. In Mexico and the United States, these workers must pay both the employee's and employer's share of social security and health benefits. In Canada they pay the

employee's and employer's share of health care and pension contributions. Although some of these costs are partially offset by tax deductions, the costs remain high for many workers in this situation. In Canada and the United States, these workers are ineligible for unemployment insurance (there is no unemployment insurance in Mexico), and they are not eligible for many other legislated employment benefits in all three countries.

Employer-Initiated Change
Some employers in North America are reducing unit labor costs through reductions in the overall

DATA ISSUES:

Working Time and Nonstandard Work

This section uses data primarily from the following household surveys:

Source	Agency
LFS, monthly	Statistics Canada
U.S. Current Population Survey monthly	U.S. Bureau of Labor Statistics
ENE	INEGI and STPS

The data for Canada are supplemented with information from the General Social Survey. The data for Mexico are supplemented with information from the National Urban Employment Survey. Changes to the U.S. Current Population Survey in 1994 reduced the number of workers classified as involuntary part-time.

Standard work hours differ significantly in each country. In Canada, legislated standard work hours vary from 40 to 48 hours per week. However, many workers in the public sector have a standard 37.5 hour work week. Overtime must be paid for work conducted beyond the standard work hours. A five-day work week is the norm. In Mexico, the legislated standard is eight hours per day with a six-day work week, or 48 hours per week, after which overtime must be paid. In the United States, the legislated stan-

dard is 40 hours per week, after which overtime pay is required. There is no legislated maximum number of hours per week. See Chapter IV for a more detailed description of employment legislation in the three countries.

Definitions of nonstandard employment vary considerably among the three countries. In Mexico and the United States, part-time work is defined as fewer than 35 hours per week, while in Canada it is defined as fewer than 30 hours per week. In Canada and the United States, part-time work data are for all jobs, while in Mexico data are for the primary job. Canada changed its definition to include the primary job only in 1995. The incidence of part-time work in the United States and Canada is often underestimated because many multiple job holders who have two part-time jobs are classified as full-time (working more than 30 hours per week), and the percentage of multiple job holders is growing. For example, in Canada in 1994, 23 percent of all jobs were part-time, although only 17 percent of workers were classified as part-time.

In Canada, "temporary" workers are defined as employees in a job with a specified end-date. This definition includes contract employees but excludes the self-employed. In Mexico, temporary workers are defined as those who have a contract for a specified period or quantity of work. In the United States, several different wage and benefit budget. One way to reduce costs is to restructure the organization to include "core" and "peripheral" workers, giving the latter group lower wages and fewer benefits. Other methods include the use of either overtime or reduced hours, irregular shifts, and downsizing, coupled with longer work hours for the remaining employees.[14]

While these arrangements provide flexibility for employers, they can also worsen working conditions. For example, frequently workers in the United States and Canada cannot refuse overtime. Nonstandard work arrangements and shift assign-

definitions of temporary workers have been used. The definition used in the analysis below, unless otherwise indicated, includes workers who expect their job will last for one year or less. It excludes both the self-employed and independent contractors. This definition is significantly narrower than the Canadian and Mexican definitions.

Definitions of "own-account self-employment" differ among the three countries. In Mexico and Canada, own-account self-employed includes both incorporated and unincorporated self-employed workers, whereas in the United States it includes only unincorporated self-employed workers—that is, those who have not set up their businesses as a legal corporation.

Different forms of nonstandard work are not mutually exclusive. On the contrary, they tend to be mutually reinforcing. At any given time, the same workers might be multiple part-time job holders, temporary part-time workers, and part-time self-employed workers.

ments that are involuntarily imposed could make balancing work and personal responsibilities more difficult for workers. Long working hours have been associated with health disorders, a higher incidence of workplace accidents, and negative social repercussions for families.[15]

Another way in which employers have reduced labor costs is by outsourcing. An example of this situation is when a former employee becomes a self-employed independent contractor and sells all of his or her production or services to the former employer. In this way, the employer becomes free of obligations such as social security and benefit payments. This situation is common in all three countries.

Several opinion polls in Canada and the United States have indicated a growing sense of job insecurity among workers in North America.[16] This insecurity may imply that although in the past workers have voluntarily changed jobs frequently, taken a part-time job or a second job, worked longer hours, or become self-employed, today more workers may be doing so at the insistence of their employers or because of difficult financial circumstances. Throughout North America, workers who have difficulty finding paid employment often turn to self-employment. Reduced job security has negative repercussions for employers as well, since workers may be less committed and less productive.

Trends in Working Time

Employment by Hours of Work in North America
As shown in Figure 26, fewer than half of North American workers had a standard 40- to 48-hour work week during 1995. Mexico had the largest percentage of workers working either fewer than 15 hours per week (7.2 percent of workers) or more than 48 hours per week (27.7 percent). A greater percentage of workers in the United States worked more than 48 hours per week (19.7 percent) than did their Canadian counterparts (14.8 percent). The United States had the most people working 40–48 hours per week and 15–34 hours

Figure 26

Employment by Hours of Work in North America
1995

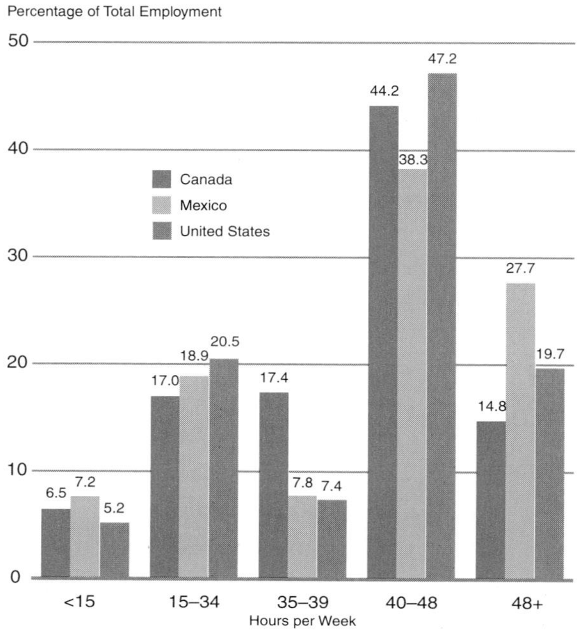

Percentage of Total Employment

Canada
Mexico
United States

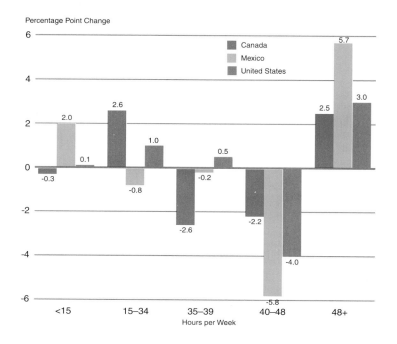

Hours per Week		
<15	6.5 / 7.2 / 5.2	
15–34	17.0 / 18.9 / 20.5	
35–39	17.4 / 7.8 / 7.4	
40–48	44.2 / 38.3 / 47.2	
48+	14.8 / 27.7 / 19.7	

Note: For Canada and Mexico, figures include workers 15 years and older; for the United States, figures include workers 16 years and older.

Source: Canada, Statistics Canada, Labour Force Survey; Mexico, STPS/INEGI, National Employment Survey; United States, Bureau of Labor Statistics, Current Population Survey.

Figure 27

Change in the Share of Employment by Hours of Work in North America
1984 and 1995

Percentage Point Change

Canada
Mexico
United States

Hours per Week	Canada	Mexico	United States
<15	-0.3	2.0	0.1
15–34	2.6	-0.8	1.0
35–39	-2.6	-0.2	0.5
40–48	-2.2	-5.8	-4.0
48+	2.5	5.7	3.0

Note: Figures span 1991 and 1995 for Mexico.

Source: Canada, Statistics Canada, Labour Force Survey; Mexico, STPS/INEGI, National Employment Survey; United States, Bureau of Labor Statistics, Current Population Survey.

per week. Canada had the most people working 35–39 hours per week; in much of the Canadian public sector, a 37.5-hour work week is standard.

There are significant gender differences in hours of work in North America. In 1995, more U.S. women worked more than 40 hours per week (57 percent of total female employment) than Mexican women (51 percent) or Canadian women (37 percent). A high percentage of men work more than 40 hours per week in all three countries: 76 percent of total male employment in the United States, 74 percent in Canada, and 73 percent in Mexico.

Change in the Share of Employment by Hours of Work in North America

Although average annual hours worked and average weekly hours did not fluctuate much in all three countries in the past decade, the averages mask growing polarization in hours of work. More North Americans are working either longer or shorter weeks than they were a decade ago.

As shown in Figure 27, the percentage of people working more than 48 hours per week grew during 1984–1995 in Canada and the United States, and during 1991–1995 in Mexico. The most rapid growth in the United States and Mexico occurred among those working more than 48 hours per week. In Canada, the most rapid growth occurred among those working more than 48 hours per week and between 15 and 34 hours per week. In Mexico, more workers worked fewer than 15 hours per week in 1995 compared with 1991. The largest decline in all three countries has been in the number of workers with 40- to 48-hour weeks.

Change in the Share of Employment by Hours of Work and Gender in North America

Figure 28 shows that during the past decade, the number of North American men working 40–48 hours per week dropped much more quickly than the number of women working those hours. More workers are putting in more than 48 hours per

Figure 28

Change in the Share of Employment by Hours of Work and Gender in North America 1984–1995

Male
Percentage Point Change

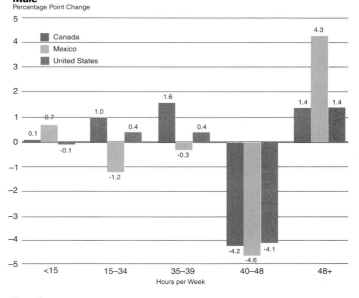

Female
Percentage Point Change

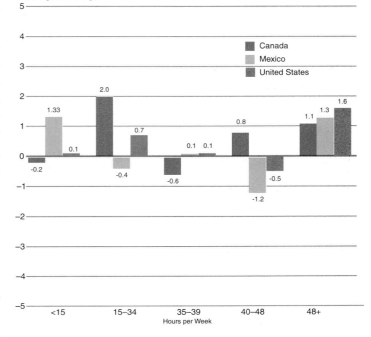

Note: Figures represent 1991–1995 for Mexico.

Source: Canada, Statistics Canada, Labour Force Survey; Mexico, STPS/INEGI, National Employment Survey; United States, Bureau of Labor Statistics, Current Population Survey.

week in all three countries. There was a particular-ly big increase in the percentage of Mexican men working more than 48 hours per week between 1991 and 1995.

In all three countries, a higher percentage of females work fewer than 35 hours per week than do males. In Mexico, 40 percent of females worked fewer than 35 hours per week in 1995, compared to 36 percent in Canada in 1995 and 35 percent in the United States in 1994. The corresponding numbers for male workers were 20 percent, 14 percent, and 19 percent, respectively, for Mexico, Canada, and the United States.

Trends in Nonstandard Work

Nonstandard Employment in North America
Nonstandard employment is growing throughout North America. It has grown in all segments of the labor market and, although it is somewhat cyclical, it has continued to increase regardless of economic conditions.

Figure 29

Nonstandard Employment in North America

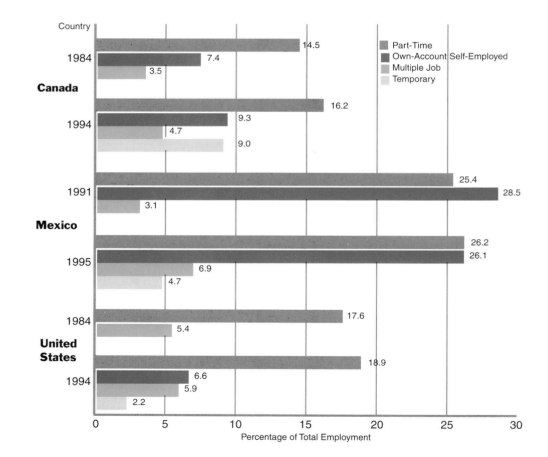

Note: For Canada and Mexico, figures include workers 15 years and older; for the United States, figures include workers 16 years and older.

Source: Canada, Statistics Canada, Labour Force Survey and General Social Survey; Mexico, INEGI, National Employment Survey; United States, Bureau of Labor Statistics, Current Population Survey.

Figure 29 shows the percentages of North American workers pursuing various nonstandard work options in 1984–1994. It is clear from the figure that the predominant form of nonstandard employment in all three countries was part-time work. In Mexico, own-account self-employment was also very common.

In all three countries, nonstandard work is concentrated in the service sector. However, it is becoming more prevalent in goods-producing sectors. A significant proportion of nonstandard work in Mexico is in the primary sector.

In Canada and the United States during 1994, more women were in nonstandard work arrangements. In Mexico in 1993, more men were in such work arrangements. However, among female workers in Mexico, a greater percentage had nonstandard work arrangements. In all three countries, women and young people occupied a disproportionately high share of part-time work during 1984–1995, whereas men occupied a disproportionate share of own-account self-employment.

Part-Time Employment in North America
As shown in Figure 30, part-time work has increased in all three countries during the 1990s. In 1995, Mexico had the highest percentage of part-time workers, 26.6 percent of all employment. In Canada and the United States, part-time workers represented 18.6 percent and 18.5 percent, respectively, of total employment as shown in Figure 31. However, if part-time work in Canada

Figure 30

Part-Time Employment in North America 1984–1995

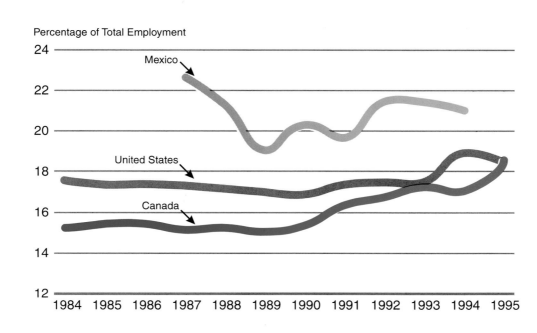

Note: Figures include part-time employment in urban areas in Mexico. For Canada and Mexico, figures include workers 15 years and older; and for the United States, figures include workers 16 years and older.

Source: Canada, Statistics Canada, Labour Force Survey; Mexico, INEGI, National Urban Employment Survey; United States, Bureau of Labor Statistics, Current Population Survey.

were defined as fewer than 35 hours per week, as it is in Mexico and the United States, rather than fewer than 30 hours per week, the percentage of part-time workers in Canada would be about 24 percent.

Part-time work in Mexican urban areas was influenced by the economic cycle as shown by the high part-time rates in 1987 and 1995 compared with other years. The increasing prevalence of part-time work is not limited to North America.

Growth in part-time jobs has outpaced growth in full-time jobs for all G7 countries except Italy.[17]

Part-Time and Full-Time Employment in North America

Voluntary part-time work is growing in all three countries, particularly in the United States and Canada. Involuntary part-time work has grown over the past decade in Canada and during the 1990s in Mexico, but has declined over the past decade in the United States. Figure 31 gives a snapshot of the three countries' full-time versus part-time employment percentages in 1995 and an earlier representative year.

Part-Time Employment by Industry in North America

As Figure 32 shows, most part-time work in North America is concentrated in the service and trade sectors. In 1994, within the United States the highest percentage of part-time workers were in the service sector and the United States had a higher percentage of part-time workers in the wholesale and retail trade sector than its North American partners. In the same year, Canada had the highest percentage of part-time workers in the service sector, in particular in community services. Mexico had the highest percentage of part-time workers in the agricultural sector in 1995.

Part-Time Employment by Gender in North America

As shown in Figure 33, part-time employees are more likely to be female in Canada and the United States, while men account for a greater share of part-time employment in Mexico, mainly because there are twice as many men in the Mexican labor force as women. However, a greater percentage of female employment is part-time, compared with the part-time share of male employment in all three countries.

Figure 31

Part-Time and Full-Time Employment in North America

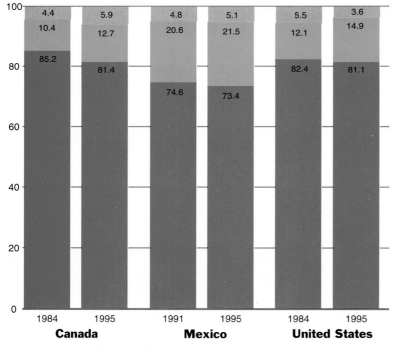

Percentage of Total Employment

■ Full-Time   ▨ Voluntary Part-Time   ▨ Involuntary Part-Time

Note: For Canada, the figures include workers 15 years and older; for Mexico, the figures include workers 12 years and older; and for the United States, the figures include workers 16 years and older.

Source: Canada, Statistics Canada, Labour Force Survey; Mexico, STPS/INEGI, National Employment Survey; United States, Bureau of Labor Statistics, Current Population Survey.

Part-time work is growing among men in the United States and Canada and among women in Mexico. The relative percentage of female workers who worked part-time remained unchanged during 1984–1995 in Canada and the United States, at 25 percent and 27 percent of female workers, respectively. The percentage of males who worked part-time grew from 7 percent to 9 percent in Canada and from 10 percent to 11 percent in the United States in the same period. In Mexico, the percentage of females who worked part-time grew from 36 percent to 41 percent during 1991–1995, while the percentage of males who worked part-time remained unchanged at 19 percent.

Part-Time Employment by Age and Gender in North America

Throughout North America, most part-time workers are prime age (25–54 years) women, in part because they need to balance work and family responsibilities. As Figure 34 shows, more part-time workers are prime-age males in Mexico (28.1 percent in 1993) than in Canada or the United States (8.9 percent and 10.7 percent, respectively, in 1994). Although a larger share of part-time workers in Mexico are young men than in Canada or the United States, 59 percent of male part-time workers in Canada and 46 percent in the United States during 1994 were under the age of 24; in Mexico in 1993, this figure was 37 percent. Many younger workers work part-time to balance work with school. The age patterns for part-time women are quite similar among the three countries.

A greater percentage of female workers than male workers hold part-time jobs involuntarily in all three countries. The gender difference is most pronounced in Canada, where in 1994, 9 percent of working women and 4 percent of working men held part-time jobs involuntarily. In Mexico in 1993, 5.8 percent of working women and 4.8 percent of working men held part-time jobs involuntarily. For the United States in 1994, the comparable numbers are 4 percent of working women and 3 percent of working men.

Comparison of Temporary Workers in North America
Temporary workers are the most difficult group to compare in North America because of differing definitions and limited data availability.[18] About 9 percent of Canadians were defined as temporary workers in 1994 compared to 8 percent in 1989. In

Figure 32

Part-Time Employment by Industry in North America 1994

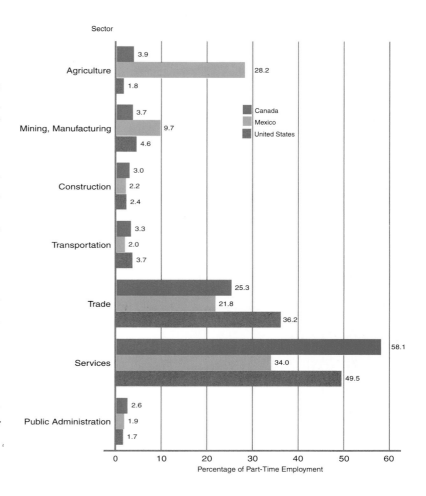

Note: Figures are 1995 for Mexico. The percentages for Mexico do not add to 100 since some respondents did not specify the industry.

Source: Canada, Statistics Canada, Labour Force Survey; Mexico, STPS/INEGI, National Employment Survey; United States, Bureau of Labor Statistics, Current Population Survey.

the United States, 2.2 percent of workers were defined as temporary in 1995. If a broader definition is used—one that includes wage and salary workers who do not expect their job to last but who may have worked for over one year in the same job, as well as self-employed workers and independent contractors—the percentage rises to 4.9 percent of total U.S. employment. In Mexico, 4.7 percent of workers were defined as temporary in 1995. In 1994, 2 percent of all employees in Canada were employed by temporary help

agencies; in the United States in 1995, 1 percent of employees worked for such agencies.

In both Canada and the United States, temporary workers were concentrated in the construction and service sectors during 1984–1995. Using the broader definition, in 1995 most temporary workers in the United States were employed in the service sector (54 percent of all temporary workers), followed by wholesale and retail trade (12 percent) and construction (10 percent) in 1995. As a percentage of total employment in a particular sector, temporary workers in Canada were concentrated in the construction (22 percent), social services (13 percent), public administration (11 percent), and other consumer services (11 percent) sectors in Canada in 1994.

In both Canada and the United States, temporary workers tend to be younger. One in six employees age 15–24 were temporary workers in Canada in 1994. Temporary workers in the United States were most concentrated in the 25–34 age group in 1995. The gender differences among temporary workers in the three countries were relatively small.

In the United States in 1995, about 43 percent of temporary workers (using the broader definition) were part-time, and 9 percent were multiple job holders. This information indicates a high degree of overlap among these forms of nonstandard work. In that same year, a majority (56 percent) of U.S. workers held temporary jobs involuntarily and said they would prefer a permanent arrangement, suggesting that this is a form of underemployment.[19]

Own-Account Self-Employment as Nonstandard Work in North America

Own-account self-employment is a predominant form of nonstandard work in Mexico, and this form of employment is growing in Canada.[20] In 1995, Mexico had the highest percentage of own-account self-employed workers in North America—26 percent of total employment; this figure was 28.5 percent in 1991. Comparable figures for Canada are 9.1 percent of total

Figure 33

Part-Time Employment by Gender in North America 1984–1995

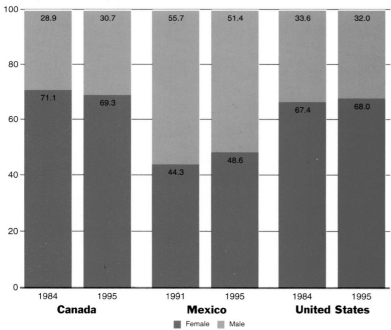

Percentage of Part-Time Employment

Female ■ Male

Note: Figures span to third quarter of 1995 for Canada and the United States. For Canada, figures include workers 15 years and older; for Mexico, figures include workers 12 years and older; and for the United States, figures include workers 16 years and older.

Source: Canada, Statistics Canada, Labour Force Survey; Mexico, STPS/INEGI, National Employment Survey; United States, Bureau of Labor Statistics, Current Population Survey.

employment in 1995, up from 7.5 percent in 1984. In the United States, unincorporated own-account self-employed workers represented 6.6 percent of all employment in January 1995, less than the comparable rate of 7.8 percent for Canada.

In Mexico and Canada, more men than women fall into the own-account self-employed category. In Mexico, 28 percent of all male workers in 1995 were self-employed and had no employees; 23 percent of all female workers met this description. In Canada, slightly more men (9 percent) than women (8 percent) fell into this category of workers in 1994; the highest percentage of male workers over the age of 55 and female workers between the ages of 45 and 54 fell into this category.

In all three countries, own-account self-employment is concentrated in the service sector. However, a large percentage of self-employment in Mexico is in the primary sector—36 percent in 1995.

Workers with Multiple Jobs in North America
A small but growing proportion of workers in all three countries are holding down more than one job at a time, with particularly rapid growth among women.[21] In 1995, Mexico had the highest rate of multiple job holders in North America, 6.9 percent of total employment. In 1994, this figure was 5.9 percent for the United States and 4.9 percent for Canada. The category had grown from 3.1 percent in Mexico in 1991, 5.4 percent in the United States in 1985, and 3.5 percent in Canada in 1984.

In Canada, women's share grew from 38.4 percent to 49 percent of all multiple job holders during 1984–1994. In the United States, this group grew from 38 percent to 46 percent of multiple job holders between 1985 and 1994. In Mexico, however, female workers' share declined from 36 percent to 22 percent of multiple job holders between 1991 and 1995.

In Mexico a greater share of male workers are multiple job holders, while in Canada a greater percentage of female workers are multiple job holders. In the United States there is no gender

Part-Time Employment by Age and Gender in North America
1994

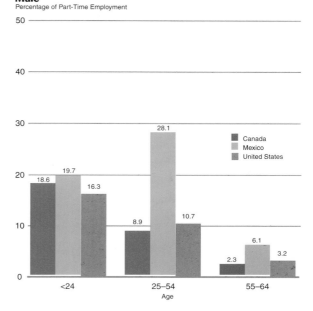

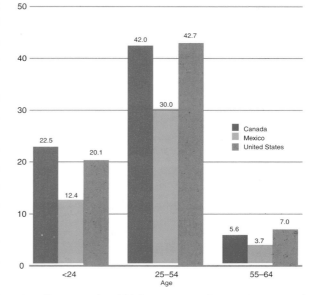

Note: Figures are for 1993 for Mexico. For Canada, figures include workers 15 years and older; for Mexico, figures include workers 12 years and older; and for the United States, figures include workers 16 years and older.

Source: Canada, Statistics Canada, Labour Force Survey; Mexico, STPS/INEGI, National Employment Survey; United States, Bureau of Labor Statistics, Current Population Survey.

difference. In all three countries, most multiple job holders were between the ages of 25 and 54 (75 percent in the United States, 73 percent in Canada in 1994, and 69 percent in Mexico in 1995).

The Knowledge-Driven Labor Market: A Higher Premium for Education and Skills

Overview

The preamble of the North American Agreement on Labor Cooperation states that the parties to the Agreement resolve to "promote, in accordance with their respective laws, high-skill, high-productivity economic development in North America by investing in continuous human resource development ... and promoting career opportunities for all workers through referral and other employment services." This statement points to the importance of life-long learning as a central element in a strategy whose goals are high job skills and high productivity.

This chapter presents comparable information on the education levels of workers; the relationship between employment, unemployment, and education; the workplace training; and the trends in employment by skill level.

The education level of workers in North America has increased substantially over the past decade. Employment growth in higher-skilled occupations is outpacing growth in lower-skilled occupations in Canada and the United States. This growth reflects a shift to the service sector and more knowledge-based industries. It is also generally agreed that competition from global labor markets is exerting pressure on workers to improve their productivity through improved skill and education. Thus, North American workers who are more educated and have higher skill levels tend to hold better paying, more stable jobs. As a consequence, one of the major labor market challenges in North America is to ensure that workers have strong initial educational qualifications and that they continuously upgrade their skills.

However, it is becoming increasingly evident that the labor market is becoming increasingly polarized on the basis of education and skill. In all three countries, workers who do not have the necessary education and skill levels to adapt to a more knowledge-based economy are more likely to be unemployed or underemployed. These workers receive fewer training opportunities in the workplace than their more skilled counterparts. Access to training is also skewed by occupation and industry in all three countries. Furthermore, as will be shown in Chapter IV, North American workers with lower education and skill levels are seeing their earnings deteriorate.

Gains in the education of the North American work force have been achieved in all three countries. Nonetheless, in both the United States and Canada more than 43 percent of employed workers had a high school degree or less education in 1994; in Mexico, this figure was 81 percent in 1995.

All three countries face a double challenge. First, they must improve the education and skill levels of unemployed and low-skilled workers to counteract increasing polarizations within the labor force between high-wage, highly skilled workers and low-wage, less-skilled workers. Second, they must provide for workers who cannot practicably join the high-wage, high-skill sector. Mexico faces the additional challenge of providing a basic education for the entire population.

Trends in Education and Training

Public Expenditures on Education in North America Figure 35 shows that Canada spends the most public funds on education as a percentage of GDP of any country in North America. However, public education expenditures as a share of GDP in Mexico grew the fastest among the three countries, from 2.9 percent to 4.5 percent of GDP during 1985–1994. Public education expenditures in the United States grew from 4.6 percent to 6.1 percent of GDP in 1984–1994, while expenditures in Canada remained steady at 7.2 percent of GDP in 1994.

When private expenditures on education are taken into account, the gap in education expenditures among Canada (8.0 percent of GDP in 1995), the United States (7.5 percent of GDP in 1994), and Mexico (6.2 percent of GDP in 1995) narrows because Mexico and the United States spend more on private education as a percentage of GDP than does Canada.

DATA ISSUES:

Education and Training

This section uses data primarily from the following sources:

Source	Agency
LFS, monthly	Statistics Canada
U.S. Current Population Survey, monthly	U.S. Bureau of Labor Statistics
National Education, Training, and Employment Survey	INEGI and STPS

The Mexican survey is a household survey conducted simultaneously with the National Employment Survey in 1993 and 1995.

The definition of education levels changed in Canada and the United States during 1984–1995. In Canada, the 1990 Labor Force Survey reclassified as "post-secondary" certain certificates that were previously unrecognized. This change accounts for some of the apparent increase in employed workers with post-secondary education. In the United States, education categories were redefined in 1992 to base education levels on the highest degree received rather than the number of years of school completed. Thus, data from 1992 and later are not directly comparable with data from earlier years. Data for 1994 onward are not directly comparable with data for 1993 and earlier because of the Current Population Survey redesign. Further, definitions of different education levels vary because, for example, years of schooling to obtain a particular degree are not homogeneous across countries or—in some cases—within countries.

There is also considerable variation in the definition of what constitutes "training." For Canada and the United States, several different sources of information on training are used, each employing its own definitions. Sources other than those mentioned here are noted in the text. Only the definitions used by government surveys are described here. Training data for Canada and the United States refer to formal training only—that is, training that is structured, is planned in advance, and has a defined curriculum. Training data for Mexico include both formal and informal training.

In Mexico, the National Education, Training, and Employment Survey defines "training" as courses received in public, private, or social training institutions, as well as in the workplace (age 12 or older). It excludes formal full-time elementary, secondary, and post-secondary education. The training did not have to occur in the year of the survey.

The Mexican Constitution requires that employers provide training to their employees. The Federal Labor Law in Mexico states that all employees have the right to receive training from their employers during work hours. Employers are required to prepare training plans that specify the training to be provided to employees at all levels in the organization. Employees are responsible for attending and otherwise meeting course requirements.

In Canada, the Adult Education and Training Survey (a household survey) defines "training" as short-term or part-time courses, apprenticeship programs, and employer-sponsored full-time programs provided to adults age 17 and over during the course of a year. It excludes regular full-time high school, college, and university students.

In the United States, the Bureau of Labor Statistics Survey of Employer Provided Training (a survey of establishments conducted in 1993) defines "training" as formal training programs that are planned in advance and that have a defined curriculum provided or financed by employers to workers age 16 and over.

Public Expenditures on Education in North America 1984–1994

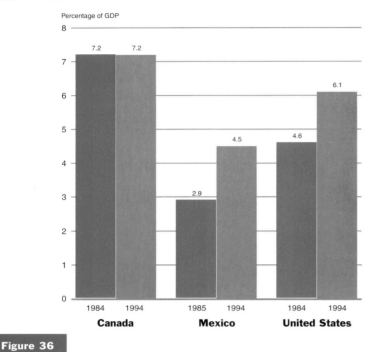

Source: Canada and United States: OECD Education at a Glance, 1995; OECD Public Education Expenditure, Costs, and Financing: An Analysis of Trends, 1970–1988. Mexico, First State of the Union Report, 1995.

Figure 36

Employment by Education Level in North America

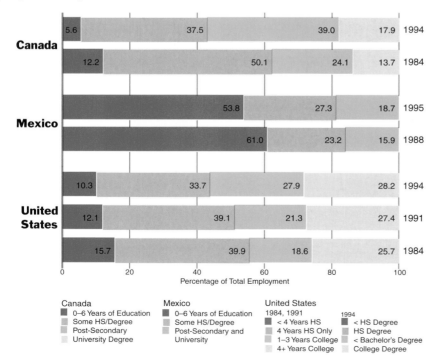

Source: Canada, Statistics Canada, Labour Force Survey; Mexico, STPS/INEGI, National Education, Training, and Employment Survey; United States, Bureau of Labor Statistics, Current Population Survey, OECD Education Database.

Employment by Education Level in North America

Employment opportunities have not been shared equally by all North American workers. Workers with low educational attainment have had consistently decreasing employment rates over the past decade in all three countries, while employment rates for more educated workers have grown. This trend is also apparent in European OECD countries.

Figure 36 illustrates how workers with varying levels of education accounted for different percentages of total employment in the three North American countries at different points in the past decade. The figure shows that in Mexico, although workers with six years or less of education still account for more than half of all employment, during 1988–1995 workers with some high school education increased from 23.2 percent to 27.3 percent of workers, and those with a post-secondary degree increased from 15.9 percent to 18.7 percent of workers. In Canada and the United States, workers with some post-secondary, college, or university education represented 56.9 percent and 56.1 percent of workers, respectively, in 1994. This number was up from 37.8 percent and 44.3 percent in 1984. In contrast, workers with a high school degree or less education dropped from 62.3 percent and 55.6 percent of Canadian and U.S. workers, respectively, to nearly 44 percent of all workers for both countries between 1984 and 1994.

Unemployment Rate by Education Level in North America

As shown in Figure 37, unemployment rates are higher for less-educated workers in Canada and the United States. In 1995, unemployment rates for workers in the United States and Canada with less than a high school degree were more than triple those for workers with a university or college degree, suggesting that there are fewer jobs for low-skilled workers and that more high-skill jobs are being created. Young, less-educated workers are particularly susceptible to high unemployment in both countries. This situation is also apparent in

Figure 37

Unemployment Rate by Education Level in North America 1995

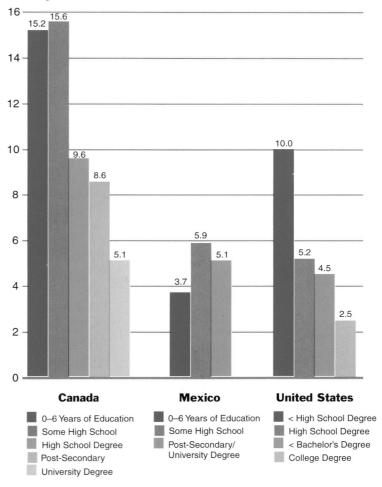

Percentage of Labor Force

Canada
- 0–6 Years of Education
- Some High School
- High School Degree
- Post-Secondary
- University Degree

Mexico
- 0–6 Years of Education
- Some High School
- Post-Secondary/ University Degree

United States
- < High School Degree
- High School Degree
- < Bachelor's Degree
- College Degree

Note: Figures span to the third quarter 1995 for Canada and the United States. Data are from 1993 for Mexico.

Source: Canada, Statistics Canada, Labour Force Survey; Mexico, STPS/INEGI, National Education, Training, and Employment Survey; United States, Bureau of Labor Statistics, Current Population Survey; *The OECD Jobs Study: Evidence and Explanations*, Paris, 1994.

OECD countries where workers with less schooling are more likely to have high unemployment rates.

Figure 37 also shows that the reverse situation was apparent in Mexico, where unemployment rates of workers with some high school or post-secondary education were higher than rates for workers with less than six years of education. This contrast could be explained by the fact that more-educated workers in Mexico can sustain a period of unemployment, while less-educated workers must work to maintain their subsistence.

Employment by Occupational Skill Level in North America

As shown in Figure 38, occupations calling for a medium level of skill are the predominant source of employment in all three countries. Canada and the United States have a higher proportion of employment in medium- and high-skill occupations, while Mexico has a higher proportion of employment in medium-skill occupations.

In Canada and the United States, the shift was from medium-skill occupations (clerical, sales, and blue-collar categories) to high-skill occupations (managerial, professional, and technical categories). Employment in low-skill occupations (services) remained relatively unchanged over the past decade. In Mexico, the shift has been from low- and high-skill occupations to medium-skill occupations during 1991–1995. Although these surveys are based on only a crude measure of skill, they do demonstrate skill shifts in the labor market.

Future growth in high-skill jobs is expected to be strong in Canada and the United States. In Canada, it is projected that 48 percent of all new jobs created between 1990 and 2000 will require more than 16 years of education and training. In the United States, the number of jobs requiring a bachelor's degree is expected to grow by 40 percent between 1992 and 2005, while jobs that do not require post-secondary education will grow by 17 percent.

Workers Who Receive Training

A greater share of workers in the United States receive training compared to their Canadian and Mexican counterparts. Training in the areas of commerce or business and technical, trades, and computers is the most common in all three countries.[22]

Workers in the United States receive more training than Canadian workers. This finding is reflected both in expenditures on training (0.6

Figure 38

Employment by Occupational Skill Level in North America
1984–1995

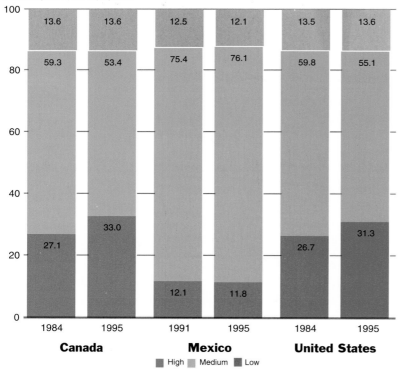

Percentage of Total Employment

| | High | Medium | Low |

Note: "High skill" includes managerial, professional, and technical occupations; "medium skill" includes clerical, sales, and blue-collar occupations; and "low skill" includes service occupations.

Source: Canada, Statistics Canada, Labour Force Survey; Mexico, INEGI, National Income and Expenditure Survey for 1984, STPS/INEGI, and National Employment Survey for 1995; United States, Bureau of Labor Statistics, Current Population Survey.

percent of GDP in the United States in 1992, compared with 0.3 percent in Canada) and in employee participation in training (42 percent of employees reported receiving training in the previous six months of 1994 in the United States, compared with 38 percent in Canada). In Mexico, 19.6 percent of employed people in 1993 reported having received training at some point.

In Canada during 1995, 70.3 percent of establishments reported offering some training (both formal and informal). In the United States during 1993, 71 percent of establishments provided formal training.

In both Canada and Mexico, most workers received training in commerce or business and in technical, trades, and computers. In the United States, training in these same fields was most commonly offered by establishments to their employees.

In Canada and the United States, a larger proportion of employed workers than of unemployed workers get training. In Mexico, one-fourth of the labor force received training at some time. Workers with higher education levels and higher incomes receive more training in all three countries, as do workers in the service sector, in larger firms, and in higher-skill occupations.[23]

In Mexico, 25.3 percent of unemployed workers in 1993 had received training at some point, compared with 19.6 percent of employed workers. In Canada, 2.8 percent of the labor force participated in 1993–1994 in federal labor market training programs for the unemployed and those at risk. In 1993, while 38 percent of employed workers in Canada received training, only 23 percent of unemployed workers were trained over the course of the year. In the United States, only 0.7 percent of the labor force participated in labor market training programs for the unemployed or at-risk worker in 1992–1993.

All three countries are in the lower tier of spending on active labor market policies (less than 1 percent of GDP) when compared with European OECD countries. This statistic is in part a result of lower unemployment rates and less long-term unemployment in North America, and therefore less spending on active labor market programs.

In all three countries, men are more likely to receive on-the-job training; women are more likely to receive other forms of training.

In North America, workers with higher education levels have higher training participation rates. In Mexico in 1993, 22.9 percent of the population of more than 12 years old and with six years or less of education received training, compared with 27.7 percent of the population with post-secondary education. In Canada in that same year, only 17 percent of workers with high school or less education participated in training, compared with 50 percent of workers who had a university degree. In the United States, workers with university qualifications are about five times more likely to receive further training than are workers with no formal qualifications. This trend is also observed in European countries.

In Canada, 59 percent of workers in the top income quintile received training in 1993, compared with 21 percent of workers in the bottom income quintile. This situation is likely to be true in the United States also because earnings and education are highly correlated, and more-educated Americans have significantly higher training rates.

In all three North American countries, training is significantly more prevalent among workers in the service sector, particularly in the fields of utilities, transport, communications; finance, insurance, real estate; and public administration. In Mexico in 1993, 15.3 percent of manufacturing workers reported that they had received training at some point, compared with 51.0 percent of workers in public administration and in health and education services; 45.0 percent of workers in finance, insurance, and real estate; and 32.0 percent of workers in utilities, transport, and communications. In Canada, 13 percent of manufacturing workers received employer-sponsored training in 1990, compared with 32 percent of workers in utilities, 18 percent in communications, 20 percent in finance, and 27 percent in public administration.

In Canada, 59 percent of workers in the top income quintile received training in 1993, compared with 21 percent of workers in the bottom income quintile.

57

In all three countries, there has been a decline in the population of workers who are covered by laws protecting the right to organize.

In the United States, the probability that an establishment provides training is higher in the finance, insurance, real estate and the transportation, communications, utilities sectors than in manufacturing.

In Canada and the United States, training is more common in medium-sized and large firms than in smaller firms. This is also the case in many OECD countries.

In Mexico in 1993, participation in training "at some point" was highest for teachers and professors (67 percent), followed by management and supervisors (56 percent), technical and professional workers (55 percent), and insurance workers (49 percent). It was lowest for agricultural occupations (3.1 percent) and construction workers (4.8 percent). In Canada in 1993, participation in formal training in establishments was highest for management and supervisors (66.5 percent), followed by professional and technical employees (59.5 percent) and by sales and customer service employees (57.3 percent). It was lowest for office and clerical workers (41.4 percent).

Unionization in North America

Overview

One of the primary objectives of the NAALC is to promote basic labor principles, including freedom of association and protection of the right to organize, the right to bargain collectively, and the right to strike. The countries resolved to encourage "strengthening labor-management cooperation to promote greater dialogue between worker organizations and employers to foster creativity and productivity in the workplace." In North America, unions provide worker representation at the workplace level on such issues as salary allocations, working conditions, and grievance resolution. Unions also provide representation at the national level on policies and legislation that protect workers' interests.

The shift in employment from the manufacturing sector to the service sector, the growth in small enterprises, and the growth in nonstandard employment have presented significant challenges to union organizing efforts in all three countries.

The main patterns that contribute to higher unionization rates in Canada than are found in the United States are successful organizing in the health, education, and public administration sectors; dramatically higher unionization rates in the construction, transportation, communications, and utilities sectors; and a slower decline in unionization in the manufacturing sector. Employment reductions in both federal and provincial public sectors, currently under way in Canada as a result of the country's high deficit, are likely to depress union membership because the Canadian public sector has the highest unionization rate. In Mexico, higher unionization than that in the United States might be explained by high levels of unionization in larger manufacturing establishments, in public sector employment, and in state-run enterprises.

In all three countries, there has been a decline in the population of workers who are covered by laws protecting the right to organize and an increase in the numbers of workers who are harder to unionize for practical reasons. In Mexico, growth in informal sector employment and in the numbers of piece workers has reduced the percentage of workers who can be organized more easily, such as wage and salary workers with a labor contract. In Canada, the number of self-employed workers who are generally not "unionizable" has grown. An exception is in the construction industry in which many self-employed workers belong to occupationally based unions. Part-time workers are more difficult to organize, as are temporary workers and workers who hold jobs for short periods of time. The higher degree of flux in the labor market—including movements between jobs and movements among employment, unemployment, and leaving the labor force—also impedes unionization.

Unionization Rate by Gender in North America
Figure 39 shows the percentages of male and female wage and salary workers who were unionized in all three Northern American countries in 1994. Unionization rates in Canada and Mexico are significantly higher than in the United States. The unionization rate in Canada was about 33 percent in 1993. The Mexican government has estimated that the unionization rate was approximately 30 percent during the 1980s. In the United States, the rate was estimated at 15.5 percent in 1995.

While unionization rates have remained relatively constant in Canada and Mexico over the past decade, they have declined substantially in the United States. Unionization rates in some OECD countries (France, Japan, Australia, the United Kingdom, Italy, and the Netherlands) have also declined in the 1980s and 1990s, while rates in other countries (Denmark, Sweden, Finland, Spain, and Germany) have remained stable or increased. The unionization rate in the federal jurisdiction in Mexico, which encompasses 22 industries including food products, textiles, chemicals, automotive, and financial sectors, was 51.4 percent in 1994, up from 45.1 percent in 1990.

Canada and the United States: Change in Unionization Rate by Gender
Figure 40 compares the rates of unionization for men and women during 1984–1994 for Canada and the United States. Canada has seen relative success in unionizing women and has had a less dramatic decline in the unionization rate of men than has been the case in the United States. The unionization rate of Canadian women increased from 27.4 percent in 1984 to 29.8 percent in 1993. The rate for women in the United States dropped from 13.8 percent to 12.9 percent between 1984 and 1995. The unionization rate of Canadian men declined slightly during 1984–1993, from 37.6 percent to 35.0 percent; the rate for men in the United States dropped sharply, from 23.0 percent to 17.9 percent, between 1984 and 1995.

Canada and the United States: Unionization Rate by Industry, and Change in Unionization Rate by Industry
Figure 41 compares the percentages of wage and salary workers in various industries who were unionized in Canada in 1992 and in the United States in 1994. Figure 42 shows the change in

Figure 39

Unionization Rate by Gender in North America

Percentage of Wage and Salary Employment

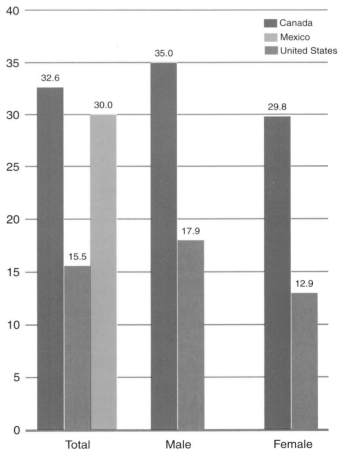

Note: The figures are 1993 for Canada, 1980s for Mexico, and 1994 for the United States.

Source: Canada, Statistics Canada, CALURA, Survey of Union Membership, and the Labour Force Survey; Mexico, N. Samaniego, "El Mercado de Trabajo Mexicano," in *Revista Mexicana del Trabajo*, Nueva época, No. 4, 5, STPS, 1994; United States, Bureau of Labor Statistics, Current Population Survey.

Figure 40

Canada and the United States: Change in Unionization Rate by Gender 1984–1994

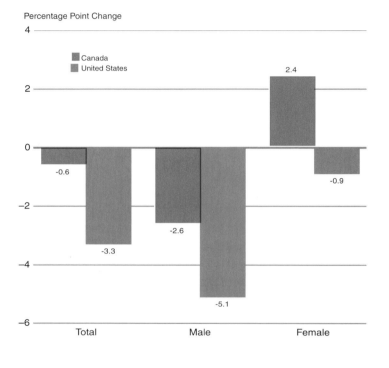

Percentage Point Change

- Canada
- United States

Total: -0.6, -3.3
Male: -2.6, -5.1
Female: 2.4, -0.9

Note: Figures are from 1993 for Canada.

Source: Canada, Statistics Canada, CALURA, Survey of Union Membership, and the Labour Force Survey; United States, Bureau of Labor Statistics, Current Population Survey.

Figure 41

Canada and the United States: Unionization Rate by Industry 1992 and 1994

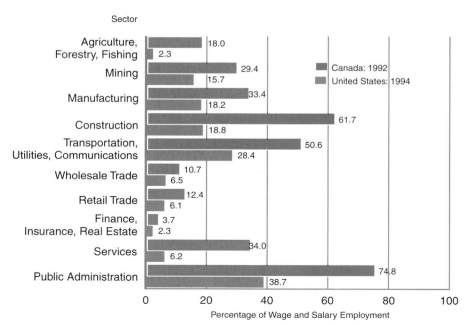

Sector

- Canada: 1992
- United States: 1994

Sector	Canada 1992	United States 1994
Agriculture, Forestry, Fishing	18.0	2.3
Mining	29.4	15.7
Manufacturing	33.4	18.2
Construction	61.7	18.8
Transportation, Utilities, Communications	50.6	28.4
Wholesale Trade	10.7	6.5
Retail Trade	12.4	6.1
Finance, Insurance, Real Estate	3.7	2.3
Services	34.0	6.2
Public Administration	74.8	38.7

Percentage of Wage and Salary Employment

Note: For Canada: In 1984 to 1992, other primary includes mining, forestry, and fishing; wholesale trade includes wholesale and retail trade. For United States: agriculture includes forestry and fishing; other primary is mining only.

Source: Canada, Statistics Canada, CALURA, and the Labour Force Survey; United States, Bureau of Labor Statistics, Current Population Survey.

unionization rates during 1984–1994 for those same industries and countries.

The relative stability in unionization rates in Canada, compared with those in the United States, reflects successful union organization efforts in the service sector in the early 1980s, particularly in the health, education, and public administration sectors, and in the construction industry. Unionization rates in public administration in Canada increased from 69.3 percent in 1984 to 74.8 percent in 1992. About 50 percent of union members in Canada in 1992 were in public administration, or in health, education, and social services. In the United States, public administration was the only sector that experienced growth in unionization rates during 1984–1994, from 35.8

percent to 38.7 percent. Unionization rates in the construction industry increased from 45.9 percent in 1984 to 61.7 percent in 1992 in Canada but declined in the United States, from 23.5 percent in 1984 to 18.8 percent in 1994.

In the transportation, communications, and utilities sectors, unionization rates have dropped in Canada (54.4 percent in 1984, compared with 50.6 percent in 1992), and more dramatically in the United States (from 38.7 percent in 1984 to 28.4 percent in 1994). In both countries, unionization in the manufacturing sector has declined. Rates dropped from 37.6 percent to 33.4 percent between 1984 and 1992 in Canada, and from 26.0 percent to 18.2 percent between 1984 and 1994 in the United States.

Figure 42

Canada and the United States: Change in Unionization Rate by Industry 1984–1994

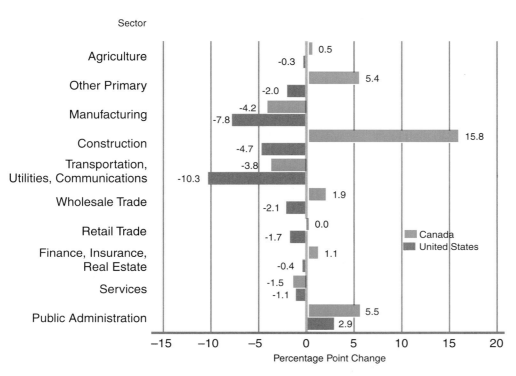

Note: For Canada: In 1984 to 1992, other primary includes mining, forestry, and fishing; wholesale trade includes wholesale and retail trade. For the United States: agriculture includes forestry and fishing; other primary is mining only.

Source: Canada, Statistics Canada, CALURA, and the Labour Force Survey; United States, Bureau of Labor Statistics, Current Population Survey.

In Mexico, 15 percent of all manufacturing establishments were unionized in 1992. In large manufacturing establishments (more than 250 workers), 87 percent had unions, compared with 84 percent of medium-sized manufacturing establishments (with 101–250 workers), 66 percent of manufacturing establishments with 16–100 workers, and 7 percent of manufacturing establishments with fewer than 16 workers. In 1992, most manufacturing jobs in Mexico (69 percent) were in large and medium-sized establishments. Unionization rates in the federal jurisdiction in 1994 were high-est in the electrical (89 percent), textile (83 percent), and hydrocarbon and petrochemical (86 percent) and lowest in rubber (20 percent), chemical (22 percent), and forestry sectors (23 percent).[24]

Canada and the United States: Union Membership by Occupation
As shown in Figure 43, more union members are in "white-collar" occupations (managerial, administrative, clerical, service, and sales) than in "blue-collar" occupations (processing, machining, construction, materials handling, transportation, and

DATA ISSUES:

Unionization

Survey Instruments

Calculating comparative union representation in the North American work force presents significant challenges to researchers. One important difference is the survey instrument used to collect the information.

In the United States, unionization data are collected through the household Current Population Survey.

In Canada, there are three main sources of unionization data: the household LFS, a survey of labor unions called CALURA, and the household Labor Market Activity Survey, which was conducted during 1986–1990. All three sources of information are used in this analysis. Data from the Labor Market Activity Survey and the LFS are probably more comparable with U.S. data because they are household surveys and they exclude unemployed unionized workers. CALURA data have been found to overstate union membership because the majority of Canadian unions include unemployed members. However, the difference in unionization rates between the two surveys is only about 2 percent.

In Mexico, unionization data for the manufacturing sector were obtained from the National Survey of Employment, Salaries, Technology and Training in the Manufacturing Sector, a survey of establishments conducted by INEGI and STPS in 1992.

Unionization rate in the federal jurisdiction from 1990 and 1994 were prepared by STPS.[a]

Calculation of Unionization Rates

Another significant difference among the three countries is the definition of elements in the work force on which to base a calculation of union penetration. In Canada, the definition of the work force that yields the percentage of union representation is paid workers, including paid agricultural workers. In 1995, these people accounted for 84 percent of the total work force. The remaining 16 percent of the work force who are excluded include self-employed and unpaid workers.

In the United States, the base includes nonagricultural wage and salary workers, including incorporated self-employed workers. This base accounted for 88 percent of total employment in 1995. Workers excluded from this base include agricultural wage and salary workers, unincorporated self-employed workers, and unpaid workers.

Mexico's unionization rates are calculated on a base of wage and salary workers who accounted for 59 percent of total employment in 1995. This base effectively removes own-account self-employed and unpaid workers, who represented 37 percent of employment in 1995, from the calculation.

primary) in both Canada and the United States. The percentage of workers in white-collar occupations in the United States increased from 55 percent in 1990 to 59 percent in 1995. In 1990, a greater percentage of union members were in white-collar occupations in Canada than in the United States (63 percent and 55 percent, respectively).

The most striking differences in the distribution of union membership by occupation between the two countries is in managerial, technical, and administrative occupations, where Canada has a significantly higher percentage of union members than the United States (33 percent and 27 percent, respectively, in 1990) and in processing, machining, and fabrication where the United States has a greater percentage of union members than Canada (27 percent and 18 percent, respectively, in 1990).

Canada and the United States: Union Membership by Age
Figure 44 shows that union membership varies significantly by age in both the United States and Canada. In both countries, union members have

Labor Law Effects

U.S. labor laws generally exclude agricultural workers, domestic employees, managers, supervisors, professional employees, confidential employees, and independent contractors from coverage of laws protecting the right to organize. With the exception of agricultural workers and the unincorporated self-employed, however, these workers are included in the "unionizable" base of the work force. It has been estimated that these workers accounted for about 40 percent of the work force in 1990.[b] Most of the 50 states prohibit collective bargaining by state employees in addition to the workers described above, although they may become union members.

Canadian law contains some of these exclusions, but in general the definitions under Canadian law permit more of these categories of workers to unionize. For example, low-level supervisors, usually excluded under U.S. law, are often covered by Canadian laws protecting the right to organize.

Mexican labor law has no specific exclusions; the right to organize is guaranteed in the Constitution. The Federal Labor Law puts a lower limit of 20 members as the size of a union but occupational unions can be formed by workers in different firms to reach this number. There has been a growing trend of employers classifying low-level supervisors, clerical workers, and others as "confidential" employees, along with managers. Confidential employees do not have the right to organize. There is also a special and growing category of piece workers (*a destajo*) not susceptible to unionization other than through their occupation.

Provincial employees in Canada and state employees in Mexico also have collective bargaining rights, unlike their counterparts in many U.S. states. Thus, the relatively low unionization rate in the United States may be understated in comparison to Canadian and Mexican rates (although this would not affect the calculation of the overall rate of decline of the unionized work force in the United States compared with changes in Canada and Mexico).

---

[a] Workers in the federal jurisdiction account for about 14 percent of total wage and salary workers. Several branches of industry in the private and public sectors are within the jurisdiction of federal labor authorities for law enforcement. The majority of private sector employees come under state jurisdiction.

[b] D. S. Cobble, "Making Postindustrial Unionism Possible," in *Restoring the Promise of American Labor Law.* Edited by S. Friedman, R. W. Hurd, R. A. Oswald, and R. L. Seeber (New York: ILR Press, 1994). Cobble's study identified categories of workers accounting for 43 percent of the work force. Removing agricultural workers and unincorporated self-employed workers who cannot effectively be unionized yields about 40 percent of the work force as part of the "unionizable" base.

Figure 43

Canada and the United States: Union Membership by Occupation
1990

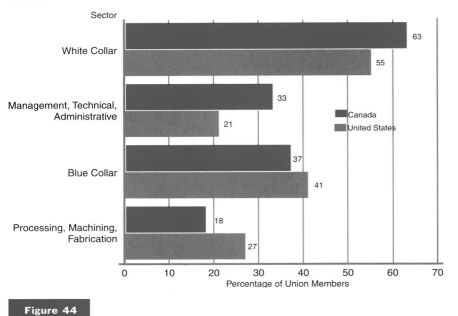

Note: White collar includes managerial, technical, administrative, clerical, service, and sales occupations. Blue collar includes processing, machining, fabricating, construction, materials handling and other crafts, transportation, and primary occupations.

Source: Canada, Statistics Canada, Survey of Union Membership and the Labour Market Activity Survey; United States, Bureau of Labor Statistics, Current Population Survey.

Figure 44

Canada and the United States: Union Membership by Age
1990

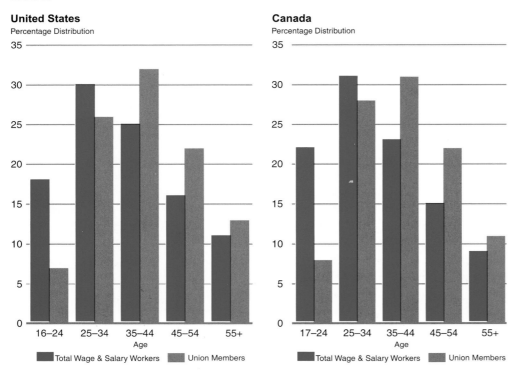

Source: Canada, Statistics Canada, Labour Market Activity Survey; United States, Bureau of Labor Statistics, Current Population Survey.

aged over the past decade compared with all wage and salary workers. Older workers represent a greater proportion of unionized workers than do younger workers, suggesting it may be more difficult to organize younger workers.

The unionization rate for 16- to 24-year-olds was 5.6 percent in the United States in 1995 and 7.9 percent in 1984. In Canada, the unionization rate for 17- to 24-year-olds declined slightly, from 20.4 percent to 19.7 percent between 1986 and 1990. In 1990, the unionization rate for 25- to 44-year-old Canadian workers was 34.6 percent, while the unionization rate for this age group in the United States was 17.0 percent. In that same year, unionization rates for workers over 45 were the highest of all age groups in both countries—37 percent for Canada and 21 percent for the United States.

Unionization rates have dropped in the United States for workers at all age levels, but the most significant drop has been for workers under the age of 35. Between 1984 and 1995, the rate for 25- to 34-year-olds dropped from 18.2 percent to 12.1 percent. Unionization rates for 35- to 44-year-olds dropped from 23.9 percent to 17.6 percent in the same period; the drop for the 45–54 age group was lower (from 25.5 percent to 21.7 percent).

In all three countries, the numbers have grown for certain types of workers who are hard to unionize or cannot be unionized. In Mexico, there has been a growth in workers in the informal sector who are hard to unionize, employees defined as "confidential" (*empleados de confianza*), and piece workers who are hard to organize (*trabajadores a destajo*). In Canada, this group includes self-employed and part-time workers.

In the United States, the numbers of part-time workers are growing but they have significantly lower unionization rates. For example, in 1995 only 7.5 percent of part-time workers in the United States were unionized, compared with 16.6 percent of full-time workers. In Canada, only 12 percent of unionized workers worked part-time, compared with 18 percent of nonunionized workers. The growth in the number of workers who remain in their jobs for less than one year—more than 20 percent of workers in all three countries—has also presented a challenge to unions.

In both Canada and the United States, unionized workers have higher salaries than do nonunionized workers. In Canada, the average hourly wage of unionized workers was C$17.53 in 1990, compared with C$13.47 for nonunionized workers. That same year, unionized workers were more than twice as likely to be covered by a pension plan than were their nonunionized counterparts (77 percent and 33 percent, respectively). In the United States in 1995, the median weekly earnings of full-time wage and salary unionized employees was U.S.$602 compared with U.S.$447 for nonunionized workers.[25]

The decline in unionized employment may be one of the factors contributing to slower wage growth. It is important to note for both countries that the differences in wages and salaries between unionized and nonunionized workers reflects variations by age, gender, education, occupation, industry, firm size, and geographic area between the two groups.

The decline in unionized employment may be one of the factors contributing to slower wage growth.

Endnotes

[1] *World Employment 1995, An ILO Report*, Geneva, 1995, p. 29, table 4.

[2] Clara Jusidman, "The Informal Sector in Mexico," Working paper no. 2, Secretariat of Labor and Social Welfare in Mexico and the U.S. Department of Labor, 1993.

[3] The underground economy consists of a wide range of economic activities and transactions inside and outside the market economy. These activities are usually unreported or unrecorded and are conducted outside of official regulations.

[4] Secretariat of Labor and Social Welfare and the United States of America, Department of Labor, "The Underground Economy in the United States," Occasional paper no. 2, September 1992, pp. 16–17.

[5] Statistics Canada, "The Size of the Underground Economy in Canada," Catalogue 13–603E, 1994.

[6] Jusidman, op. cit. In this study the informal sector is measured according to different definitions. The data

presented refer to the definition that includes household domestic work, employees, employers, and piece workers in establishments with fewer than five workers, excluding sectors usually defined as formal self-employed, excluding professionals and unpaid workers.

[7] In-bond industries (*maquiladora*) refer to firms that are located in national territory and that establish a contract to process or assemble components and machinery temporarily imported and to re-export them thereafter. Not all inputs are imported. Around 2 percent are national inputs.

[8] "Insurance employees" refers to salaried, permanent workers covered by the IMSS. These data are generally used to measure employment in the private formal sector. In 1988, permanent workers covered by the IMSS accounted for around 43 percent of total wage and salary workers.

[9] The National Income and Expenditure Survey of 1984 found that the number of unpaid family workers represented 9.5 percent of total employment. In 1988 the National Employment Survey (ENE) found this category at 14.4 percent of total employment.

[10] Definitions of "own-account self-employment" differ among the three countries. In Mexico and Canada, the category "own-account self-employed" includes both in-corporated and unincorporated self-employed workers, whereas in the United States, it includes only unincorporated self-employed workers—that is, those who have not set up their business as a legal corporation.

[11] Report of the Advisory Group on Working Time and the Distribution of Work, Human Resources Development Canada, Ottawa, 1994.

[12] K. McMullen, *Skill and Employment Effects of Computer-Based Technology: The Results of the Working with Technology Survey III*, Canadian Policy Research Networks, Ottawa (forthcoming).

[13] *Report of the Advisory Group on Working Time*, op. cit.

[14] Some evidence shows that downsizing may not increase productivity. See, for instance, G. Betcherman, K. McMullen, N. Leckie, and C. Caron, *The Canadian Workplace in Transition*, IRC Press, Queen's University, 1996.

[15] See Betcherman et al. See also V. R. Fuchs and J. P. Jacobsen, "Employee Response to Compulsory Short-Time Work," in *Industrial Relations* 30, no. 3, 1991, pp. 501–13; and J. B. Schor, *The Overworked American*, New York: HarperCollins, 1993.

[16] "Decima Workplace Survey in Canada," Decima, 1992; and *USA Today* Poll, 1995.

[17] *International Labor Comparisons in G–7 Countries: A Chart Book*, U.S. Department of Labor, 1994.

[18] Some of the data supporting this discussion of temporary workers come from Statistics Canada's General Social Survey and Labor Force Survey and the U.S. Bureau of Labor Statistics' Supplement to the U.S. Current Population Survey dated February 1995.

[19] For a definition of underemployment, see Chapter III.

[20] The data supporting this discussion of own-account self-employment come from Statistics Canada's General Social Survey and Labor Force Survey, from Mexico's INEGI and the STPS National Employment Survey, and from the U.S. Bureau of Labor Statistics' U.S. Current Population Survey.

[21] The data supporting this discussion of multiple job holders come from Statistics Canada's General Social Survey and Labor Force Survey, from Mexico's INEGI and the STPS National Employment Survey, and from the U.S. Bureau of Labor Statistics' U.S. Current Population Survey.

[22] The data supporting this discussion of training shares and training areas come from G. Betcherman, N. Leckie, and K. McMullen, *Developing Skills in the Canadian Workplace: The Results of the Ekos Workplace Training Survey*, Ottawa: Canadian Policy Research Networks (forthcoming); OECD and Statistics Canada, *Literacy, Economy, and Society: Results from the First International Adult Literacy Survey*, 1995; and David Stambrook, "On-the-Job Training and Organizational Effectiveness," *Labor Force Development Review*, Research report 6, Ottawa, Canadian Labor Force Development Board, 1993.

[23] The data supporting this discussion of who gets training come from the OECD *Employment Outlook*, 1994 and 1995; *The OECD Jobs Study—Evidence and Explanations: Employment in Europe*, European Commission, 1995; and Canadian Policy Research Networks Inc., "Workplace Training Survey," 1996.

[24] National Survey of Employment, Salaries, Technology, and Training in the Manufacturing Sector, 1992, INEGI, STPS, and "Employed and Unionized Workers in the Industrial Sector of the Federal Jurisdiction," March 1996, STPS.

[25] The data supporting the discussions of hard-to-unionize workers and comparative salaries come from CALURA and the Labor Market Activity Survey, the INEGI National Employment Survey, and the U.S. Bureau of Labor Statistics' U.S. Current Population Survey.

CHAPTER III

Employment Security Issues: Multiple Dimensions of Unemployment, Underemployment, and Job Insecurity

Overview

This chapter describes the different manifestations and multiple dimensions of unemployment, underemployment, and job insecurity in an effort to provide a broader understanding of certain labor market conditions faced by workers in North America. These conditions are frequently labeled as the "underutilization of labor," "hidden unemployment," and "marginal employment." They are often defined differently by various countries and researchers.

In recent years, governments and research organizations in North America and elsewhere, as they grapple with social and economic change, have attempted to develop a better picture of these conditions. There are many dimensions to unemployment, underemployment, and job instability, and their relative importance differs for each country in North America.

Unemployment rates in Canada are the highest in North America, and they decreased during 1984–1995. In Mexico, rates remained low by North American standards but increased sharply in 1995. Rates have dropped in the United States during 1984–1995. Throughout North America, unemployment rates for young people are significantly higher than for other workers, the incidence of unemployment (the percentage of people in the labor force who become unemployed in a given period) is high, and a significant portion of workers have jobs lasting one year or less. These factors point to a higher degree of job flux in North America, particularly among young workers, compared with other Organisation for Economic Co-operation and Development (OECD) countries. However, young workers in other OECD countries have higher unemployment rates than in North America.

Unemployment rates for women were higher than unemployment rates for men in the 1980s. However, in the 1990s, unemployment rates for men rose more rapidly than those for women both in Canada and in the United States; thus unemployment rates stayed higher for men than for women during most of 1990–1995. In Mexico, unemployment for women increased more rapidly than unemployment for men, which caused slightly higher unemployment rates for women than for men in the 1990s.

The reasons why workers become unemployed will vary considerably from country to country. Canada and Mexico have a larger proportion of unemployed workers who lose their jobs than does the United States because a significantly larger proportion of unemployed workers in the United

Throughout North America, a significant portion of workers have jobs lasting one year or less.

States are labor force reentrants. The proportion of unemployed workers who lost their jobs has grown in Canada, Mexico, and the United States since 1988.

Commonly cited factors that make many workers in North America feel insecure about their jobs include the combination of the growth in the duration and incidence of unemployment, involuntary nonstandard work, poorly paid work, and short-tenure jobs. The reasons frequently given for increased workplace restructuring include

technological advances, intensified global competition (partly caused by more liberalized trade), and changing skill requirements. This restructuring has been associated with less access to secure income, benefits, training, and promotions. While the effect is felt most among workers who lose their jobs, it is also felt by those who remain in their jobs—the "survivors" of workplace reorganizations or downsizing. These latter workers often fear the next round of cuts, increased workloads, and growing pressure to work longer hours to compensate

DATA ISSUES:

Unemployment and Underemployment

This section uses data primarily from the following household surveys:

Source	Agency
LFS, monthly	Statistics Canada
U.S. Current Population Survey, monthly	U.S. Bureau of Labor Statistics
ENE	INEGI and STPS

The data for Mexico are supplemented with information from the National Urban Employment Survey. Mexican unemployment data for nonsurvey years for the entire country were estimated, taking into account unemployment trends from the National Urban Employment Survey and economic behavior during 1984–1995. The coverage of the National Urban Employment Survey expanded from 12 to 39 urban areas during this period; by 1995, the urban survey covered 43 percent of total employment in Mexico and 92 percent of total employment in urban areas. It excluded workers living in areas with populations of fewer than 100,000. Changes to the U.S. Current Population Survey in 1994 increased the unemployment rate and reduced the number of people classified as discouraged workers.

Differences in definitions of unemployment among the three countries are significant. In the United States, unemployed

workers are defined as those age 16 and over who are without a job that provides at least one hour of work per week and who have looked for work in the past four weeks; those who are expecting to be recalled from layoff, whether or not they have engaged in job-seeking activity; or those who are waiting to start a new job within 30 days. So called "passive" job hunters, such as those who merely read help-wanted advertisements, are not considered to be in the labor force. As of January 1994, workers waiting to begin a new job had to look for work within the preceding four weeks to be considered unemployed.[a]

The definition of unemployed workers in Canada is generally similar to that in the United States, with the following notable exceptions: unemployed workers age 15 years and older are included, workers who do not look for a job but who expect to be recalled or to begin a new job within the four weeks are considered unemployed, and passive job hunters are counted as unemployed. Statistics Canada has estimated that this last distinction accounted for almost one-fifth of the difference between unemployment rates in Canada and the United States in 1993.

In Mexico, unemployed workers are defined as people 12 years of age and older who are without a job that provides at least one hour of work per week and who have looked for work within the preceding four weeks. Workers who did not look for work within the preceding four weeks but who looked for work within the

for the reduced number of workers in their workplace.[1]

Unemployment Rate in North America

Overall unemployment levels in North America dropped from 11.0 million workers in 1984 to 10.5 million workers in 1995, and the North American unemployment rate decreased from 7.4 percent to 5.8 percent during that period. This rate is lower than the average for all OECD countries; in 1995, 34.5 million people, or some 7.6 percent of the

OECD labor force, were unemployed. It is also significantly lower than the unemployment rate in Central and Western Europe (9.2 percent in 1995).[2]

As shown in Figure 45, Canada had the highest unemployment rate in North America during 1984-1995, followed by the United States and Mexico. Unemployment in Canada has ratcheted up over successive cycles, resulting in increases over time in the aggregate rate. In the United States, fluctuations in unemployment have mainly been

---

preceding two months are considered unemployed if they are going to start a new job in less than three months. Workers who expected to be recalled or to start a new job within four weeks are considered employed. When unemployment rates in Mexican urban areas were adjusted to U.S. concepts, the rate increased from 3.1 percent to 5.1 percent in 1993.[b]

Behavioral differences among workers are also significant. It has been found, for example, that nonworking Canadians are more likely to keep searching for work than are their U. S. counterparts and thus remain unemployed rather than leaving the labor force. Affordability is another important consideration. In Mexico real earnings have dropped, severance pay is limited to salary workers, and there is no unemployment insurance, so many Mexican workers cannot "afford" to be unemployed. These workers find at least one hour of work per week through self-employment or other means, and are thus considered employed. Higher savings rates and more generous unemployment insurance benefits in Canada may allow workers to search for work longer than U.S. and Mexican workers.

Definitions of discouraged and involuntary part-time workers vary across countries. Discouraged workers are those who have given up looking for work and are no longer considered in the labor force. To be considered discouraged, workers must have sought work within the preceding year in the United States and

within the preceding six months in Canada; no time period is specified in Mexico. In Canada and the United States, involuntary part-time workers are defined as those who could find only part-time work. The redesign of the U.S. Current Population Survey in 1994 added two questions for those who could find only part-time work: "Do you want full-time work?" and "Are you available to take full-time work?" This distinction reduced the percentage of workers classified as involuntary part-time. In Mexico, involuntary part-time workers are defined as those who work part-time because of reductions in production or sales that occurred as a result of a slowdown in economic activity or weather conditions. The ILO defines involuntary part-time and temporary workers, as well as those who underuse their skills or are paid abnormally low salaries, as underemployed.[c]

---

[a] "How Government Measures Unemployment," U.S. Bureau of Labor Statistics, 1994.

[b] S. Fleck and C. Sorrentino, "Employment and Unemployment in Mexico's Labor Force," Monthly Labor Review, U.S. Department of Labor, November 1994.

[c] International Labor Organization, "Surveys of the Economically Active Population: Employment, Unemployment, and Underemployment," an ILO manual on concepts and methods.

cyclical. In Mexico, unemployment rates declined between 1984 and 1991 and rose slightly thereafter through 1994. The rate rose sharply in 1995 as a result of the economic crisis.

Only about half of unemployed workers in Canada in 1994 and 35 percent of workers in the United States from March 1995 to March 1996 received unemployment insurance benefits.

Unemployment Rate by Age and Gender in North America

Figure 46 shows that in 1995, unemployment rates among young people (under 25 years of age) were more than double those of other workers in North America. Young men had the highest unemployment rates in Canada and the United

States, and young women had the highest unemployment rate in Mexico. Higher unemployment rates among youth are partly due to the fact that they frequently obtain temporary work arrangements as they transition from school to work.

Unemployment rates for young men and women rose, compared to other age groups, in 1984–1995 throughout North America. In all three countries, workers over the age of 45 had the lowest rates of unemployment in 1995.

Unemployment Rate by Gender in North America

Figure 47 compares Canada, Mexico, and the United States in terms of unemployment rates for men and women during 1984–1995. The figure shows that in 1984–1989, women had higher

Figure 45

Unemployment Rate in North America 1984–1995

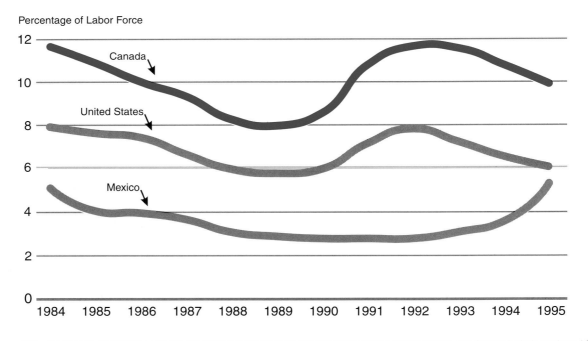

Note: For Canada and Mexico, the figures include workers 15 years and older, for the United States, the figures include workers 16 years and older.

Source: Canada, Statistics Canada, Labour Force Survey; Mexico, INEGI, National Income and Expenditure Survey for 1984, and STPS/INEGI, National Employment Survey with estimated data for non-survey years; United States, Bureau of Labor Statistics, Current Population Survey.

unemployment rates than men in all three countries. The recession in Canada and the United States in 1990–1991 had a greater impact on working men, however, and their unemployment rates surpassed those of women during 1991–1994. In 1995, unemployment rates for Canadian men remained higher than those for Canadian women, while in the United States the female rate was slightly higher. Unemployment rates for women remained higher than those of men in Mexico in 1991–1995, although the gender gap narrowed considerably.

Duration of Unemployment in North America
Figure 48 shows that during 1984–1995, Canadian workers stayed unemployed longest, followed by U.S. workers and those in urban areas in Mexico. The fact that the duration of unemployment in

Figure 46

Unemployment Rate by Age and Gender in North America 1995

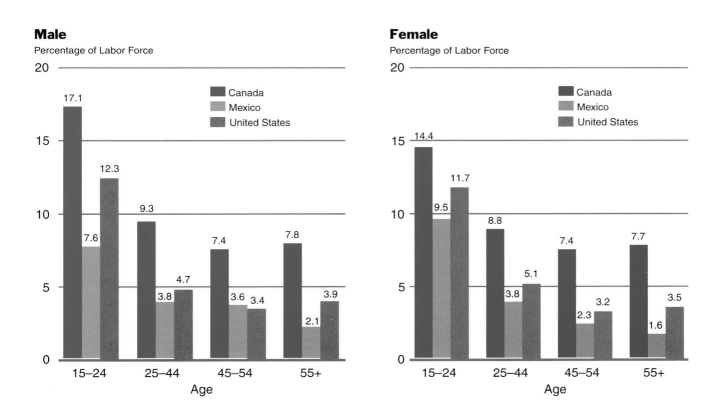

Male

Percentage of Labor Force

Canada
Mexico
United States

Age	15–24	25–44	45–54	55+
Canada	17.1	9.3	7.4	7.8
Mexico	7.6	3.8	3.6	2.1
United States	12.3	4.7	3.4	3.9

Female

Percentage of Labor Force

Canada
Mexico
United States

Age	15–24	25–44	45–54	55+
Canada	14.4	8.8	7.4	7.7
Mexico	9.5	3.8	2.3	1.6
United States	11.7	5.1	3.2	3.5

Note: Figures span to second quarter 1995 for Canada and to third quarter 1995 for the United States, 16–24 age group.

Source: Canada, Statistics Canada, Labour Force Survey; Mexico, STPS/INEGI, National Employment Survey; United States, Bureau of Labor Statistics, Current Population Survey.

Figure 47

Unemployment Rate by Gender in North America 1984–1995

Canada
Percentage of Labor Force

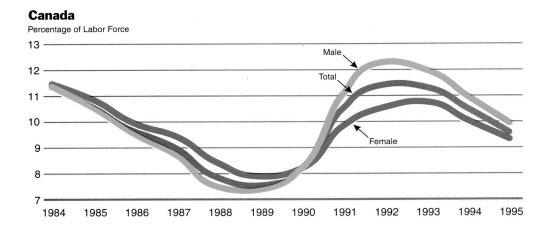

Mexico
Percentage of Labor Force

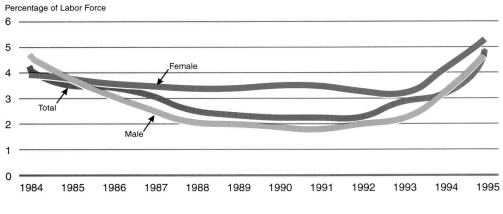

United States
Percentage of Labor Force

Note: For Canada and Mexico, figures include workers 15 years and older; for the United States, figures include workers 16 years and older.

Source: Canada, Statistics Canada, Labour Force Survey; Mexico, STPS/INEGI, National Employment Survey 1991, 1993, 1995, and INEGI, National Income and Expenditure Survey, 1984, with estimated data for non-survey years; United States, Bureau of Labor Statistics, Current Population Survey.

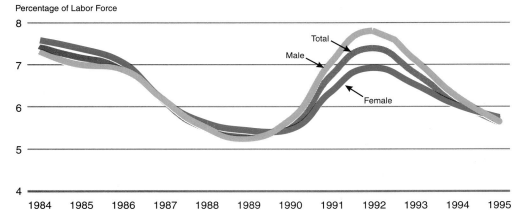

Mexico did not increase in 1995, while real earnings dropped substantially and employment in retail trade rose, suggests that unemployed workers took lower paying jobs in the informal sector.

In 1995, 13.8 percent of unemployed Canadian workers were unemployed for more than a year, and 27.1 percent were unemployed for more than six months. In the United States that year, 9.7 percent of unemployed workers were unemployed for more than a year, and 17.3 percent were unemployed longer than six months. In Mexico, 1.5 percent of urban workers were unemployed for more than a year and 7.9 percent were unemployed for more than six months. The incidence of long-term unemployment is significantly higher in European OECD countries than in North America; more than 30 percent of workers tend to be unemployed

for more than one year in most European countries.[3] In Canada and the United States, workers over the age of 45 stayed unemployed longer than Canadian and U.S. workers in other age groups.

In Canada, 24 percent of the labor force experienced unemployment in 1993, compared with 15 percent of the U.S. labor force in the same year and 15–20 percent of the Mexican labor force in 1991.[4] Thus unemployment touches a significant proportion of the work force in North America. This experience may contribute to the job insecurity felt by many workers.

Unemployed Job Leavers and Job Losers in North America

Workers who become unemployed either lose their jobs or leave their jobs. Figure 49 compares the

Figure 48

Duration of Unemployment in North America 1984–1995

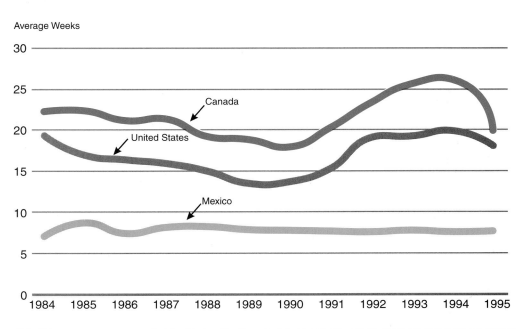

Average Weeks

Note: Urban areas are represented for Mexico. For Canada, figures include workers 15 years and older; for Mexico, figures include workers 12 years and older; and for the United States, figures include workers 16 years and older.

Source: Canada, Statistics Canada, Labour Force Survey; Mexico, INEGI, National Urban Employment Survey; United States, Bureau of Labor Statistics, Current Population Survey.

percentages for North American workers who lost their jobs and those who left their jobs in 1984–1995. Most unemployed workers had lost their jobs in the United States in 1995 (89 percent), in Canada in 1994 (84 percent), and in urban areas in Mexico in 1995 (60 percent). The proportion of unemployed workers who lost their jobs increased in all three countries in 1989–1995.

In Mexican urban areas during 1994–1995, unemployed workers who lost their jobs for economic reasons grew rapidly, from 50 to 60 percent, reflecting the worsening economic situation.

Canada, Mexico, and the United States differ significantly in terms of reasons for unemployment. In 1995, 57 percent of all unemployed workers at the national level in Mexico had lost their jobs or had been temporarily laid off, compared with 55 percent in Canada and 48 percent in the United States. Of all unemployed workers in the United States in 1995, 35 percent were reentering the labor force, compared with 25 percent in

Figure 49

Unemployed Job Leavers and Job Losers in North America
1984–1995

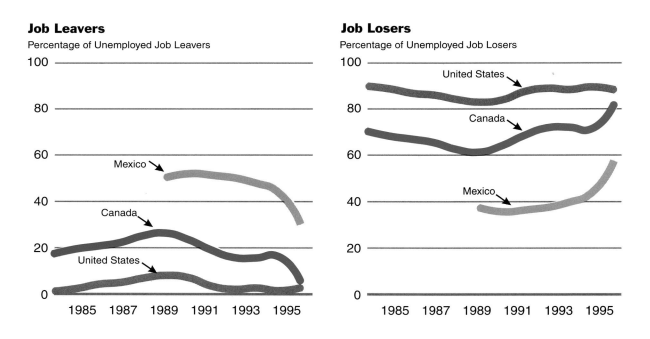

Job Leavers
Percentage of Unemployed Job Leavers

Job Losers
Percentage of Unemployed Job Losers

Note: For Canada, figures include workers 15 years and older; for Mexico, figures are for urban areas and include workers 12 years and older; and for the United States, figures include workers 16 years and older.

Source: Canada, Statistics Canada, Labour Force Survey; Mexico, INEGI, National Urban Employment Survey; United States, Bureau of Labor Statistics, Current Population Survey.

Canada. New entrants represented 12 percent of all unemployed workers in Mexico in 1995, compared with 8 percent in the United States in 1995 and 5 percent in Canada in 1994.

*Work Experience of the Unemployed
in North America*
As Figure 50 shows, Canada has the highest percentage of experienced unemployed workers (job losers, job leavers, and reentrants) in North America, followed by the United States and

Mexico. The figure also shows that during 1984–1995, there was rapid growth in the numbers of experienced, unemployed workers in Mexican urban areas. This growth was in part due to the economic slowdown, the fact that the average age of workers is increasing in that country, and the slowing employment growth. Experienced, unemployed workers have also increased in the United States. This growth may suggest that experienced workers in these countries are having more trouble finding employment.

Figure 50

Work Experience of the Unemployed in North America 1984–1995

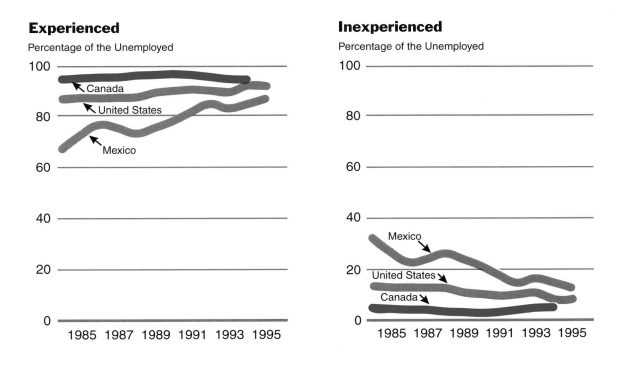

Experienced

Percentage of the Unemployed

Inexperienced

Percentage of the Unemployed

Note: Urban areas are represented for Mexico. For Canada, figures include workers 15 years and older; for Mexico, figures include workers 12 years and older; and for the United States, figures include workers 16 years and older. "Experienced" is defined as job losers, job leavers, and reentrants; "inexperienced" includes new entrants.

Source: Canada, Statistics Canada, Labour Force Survey; Mexico, INEGI, National Urban Employment Survey; United States, Bureau of Labor Statistics, Current Population Survey.

Figure 51

Unemployment Rate and Complementary Employment Indicators in North America 1984–1995

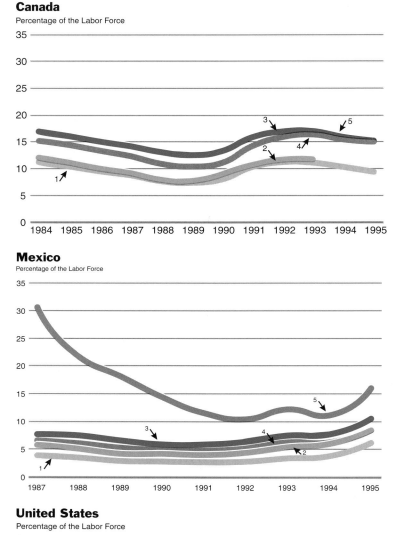

Canada
Percentage of the Labor Force

1
Persons
Unemployed

2
Persons Unemployed
and Discouraged
Workers

3
Persons Unemployed
and Persons Working
<15 Hours/Week

4
Persons Unemployed
and Part-Time Workers
for Economic Reasons

5
Persons Unemployed
and Minimum-Wage
Workers

Mexico
Percentage of the Labor Force

Note: Urban areas are represented for Mexico.

Source: Canada, Statistics Canada, Labour Force Survey, and the OECD *Employment Outlook*, 1995; Mexico, INEGI, National Urban Employment Survey; United States, Bureau of Labor Statistics, Current Population Survey.

United States
Percentage of the Labor Force

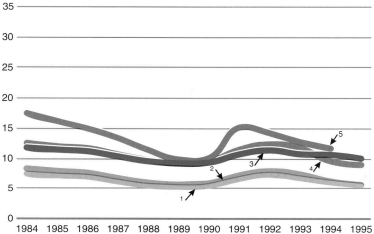

Complementary Indicators of Employment and Unemployment in All Three Countries

Unemployment is one indicator of adverse labor market conditions. The complementary indicators of employment can signal the presence of other potentially adverse conditions in the labor market in each country. The complementary indicators are not mutually exclusive. For example, a person earning the minimum wage might also be working fewer than 15 hours per week. Figure 51 attempts to show the relationship among some of these indicators in North America during 1984–1995.

In Canada, a high unemployment rate and longer durations of unemployment are the main indicators of adverse labor market conditions. Involuntary part-time work and people working fewer than 15 hours per week are important indicators. Each of these measures adds 5–6 percentage points to the measured unemployment rate.

In Mexico, the percentages of urban workers earning the minimum wage and workers working fewer than 15 hours per week are indicators of labor market difficulty, thereby adding 7 percentage points and 3 percentage points, respectively, to the measured urban unemployment rate for 1995. The indicator that takes into account minimum-wage workers in Mexico was more sensitive to the economic cycle than was the unemployment rate during 1987–1995.

Mexico has a higher percentage of discouraged workers than either the United States or Canada; these workers added about 2 percentage points to the measured unemployment rate in 1987–1995. Women between the ages of 55 and 64 years were the most likely to be discouraged workers (7.0 percent of this group were discouraged workers in 1993), followed by women between the ages of 16 and 24 years (3.7 percent in 1993).

In the United States, involuntary part-time work and workers working fewer than 15 hours per week are important indicators of weak labor market conditions, thus adding 4.7 and 3.5 percentage points, respectively, to the measured unemployment rate in 1994. The percentage of workers earning the minimum wage may be indicative of weak conditions and added 5.8 percentage points to the unemployment rate in 1994.

The sharp growth among minimum-wage workers in the United States in 1991 is partly the result of an increase in the minimum wage in that year.

Job Tenure in North America

The United States has a higher proportion of short-tenure jobs than does Canada or Mexico. In 1991, 29 percent of total employment in the United States, compared with 25.3 percent in Mexico in 1993 and 22.2 percent in Canada in 1991, was in jobs with tenures of one year or less. This North American pattern is significantly higher than that of other OECD countries (the corresponding percentages were 15.7 percent for France, 12.8 percent for Germany, and 9.8 percent for Japan in 1991).[5]

Figure 52 compares average job durations as percentages of total employment in the three North American countries in the early 1990s. The figure shows that more than 44.4 percent of total employment in the United States in 1991 was in jobs with tenures of less than 10 years. The corresponding numbers for Mexico and Canada were 47.1 percent in 1993 and 47.9 percent in 1991.

Average job tenure increased slightly in Canada and the United States during 1979–1993. In 1993, the average Canadian worker had spent 7.9 years in a job, compared with 6.7 years for the average worker in the United States. This is higher than the 1979 figures for these countries (7.3 and 6.4 years, respectively) but significantly lower than in other OECD countries, where tenures of more than 10.0 years are common.

Despite increases in average job tenure, job turnover is increasing in Canada and the United States. During 1978–1992 in Canada, the average job gain rate between consecutive years was 13.4 percent and the job loss rate was 12.1 percent.[6] In the United States, the proportion of workers with strong stability (those who changed employers no more than once in the decade) dropped from 67 percent of workers in the 1970s to 52 percent in

The United States has a higher proportion of short-tenure jobs than does Canada or Mexico.

the 1980s; the percentage of workers with weak stability (those who changed employers in four or more years of the decade) doubled from 12 percent in the 1970s to 24 percent in the 1980s. (The data are for prime-age male adults who were 24–48 years old at the beginning of the decade).[7]

Endnotes

[1] "Technological and Organizational Change and Labor Demand/Flexible Enterprise: Human Resource Implications," Applied Research Branch, Human Resources Development Canada, 1996.

[2] OECD. *Employment Outlook*, 1996.

[3] Ibid.

[4] OECD. *Employment Outlook*, 1995. Ana Revenga and Michelle Riboud, "Unemployment in Mexico: Analysis of Its Characteristics and Determinants," World Bank, 1992. Data for Mexico are not directly comparable with the other two countries because Mexico's definition of open unemployment included people who were not in the labor force, but who were not studying, nor taking care of the household, nor retired, nor disabled. The rationale for including these people as unemployed is that in Mexico, one-fourth of unemployment periods for men and over half of unemployment periods for women end when the individual withdraws from the labor force, and a large fraction of those who withdraw reenter the labor force within three months.

[5] OECD. *Employment Outlook*, 1993.

[6] G. Picot, J. Baldwin, and R. Dupuy. "Working Paper Series 71," Statistics Canada, 1994.

[7] National Commission for Employment Policy, based on University of Michigan's Panel Study of Income Dynamics.

Figure 52

Job Tenure in North America

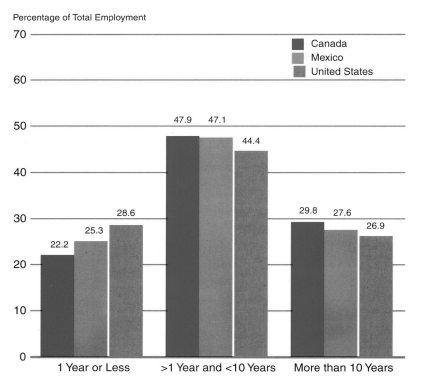

Percentage of Total Employment

Legend: Canada, Mexico, United States

Data values:
- 1 Year or Less: 22.2, 25.3, 28.6
- >1 Year and <10 Years: 47.9, 47.1, 44.4
- More than 10 Years: 29.8, 27.6, 26.9

Note: The data are for the year 1993 for Mexico and 1991 for Canada and the United States. For Canada, the figures include workers 15 years and older; for Mexico, the figures include workers 12 years and older; and for the United States, the figures include workers 16 years and older.

Source: Canada and United States: OECD *Employment Outlook*, 1993; Mexico, STPS/INEGI, National Education Training and Employment Survey.

CHAPTER IV

Earnings, Productivity, Income Distribution, and Employment Benefits

Major issues in today's rapidly changing North American economy include the relationships among salaries and benefits, the growth of employment and labor productivity, and the distribution of income. This chapter presents basic data on these issues. The analysis is based on information published by Canada, Mexico, and the United States. The sources used for each country vary and present distinct coverage as well as conceptual and methodological differences (see the various screened boxes titled Data Issues in each chapter of this book). Given these differences among the three countries, the following presentation focuses on the trends of earnings, productivity, income distribution, and employment benefits in each country rather than on a comparison of those variables among North American countries.

Trends in Earnings

Overview

Among the major findings, real earnings for full-time wage and salary workers in the private sector grew at a lower rate than labor productivity throughout 1984–1995 in the United States. Real earnings for all employees at the national level in Canada remained virtually unchanged, while labor productivity grew by 9.7 percent during 1984–1995. In Mexico, earnings for wage and salary workers in the private formal sector recovered their growth rate after 1989 mainly because of a reduction in inflation as well as an increase in labor productivity growth. Real earnings fell sharply in Mexico after the peso devaluation at the end of 1994. This change was mainly a result of moderate wage increases caused by the implementation of a strict monetary stabilization policy.

During 1984–1995, the three countries had significant inequality of earnings among industrial sectors and among workers. Earnings differences were observed among workers according to gender and levels of education, although gender differences have been reduced. There is evidence that the earnings gap between men and women is reduced as their education levels increase, although for a complete analysis it is important to take into account other factors such as sector, occupation, and hours worked. This situation has been observed in all European OECD countries in which women have generally achieved larger increases in real earnings than men, not only because of a rise in the earnings of more qualified women, but also because of a greater growth in wages of women than in wages of men.[1] Throughout North

Real earnings fell sharply in Mexico after the peso devaluation at the end of 1994.

DATA ISSUES:
Earnings and Employment

Sources of Information

For Canada, the main source of information on average weekly earnings was the Survey of Employment, Payrolls, and Hours (SEPH), which is designed to measure the monthly levels and trends of payroll employment, paid hours, and earnings in firms of all sizes.

For the United States, median earnings data for full-time wage and salary workers came from the Current Population Survey. Earnings data by industry came from the Current Employment Statistics (CES) Survey, which is a monthly survey of business establishments and provides estimates on employment, hours, and earnings at the national level. The CES Survey covers all industries except agriculture.

Mexico does not have a specific survey of earnings. However, alternative sources of information such as the Monthly Industrial Survey, the *Maquiladora* Survey, and the Trade Establishments Survey provide data on earnings. Only the *Maquiladora* Survey provides data at the national level. The Economic Census provides information every five years. Earnings data reported by enterprises that are registered at the Mexican Institute of Social Security (IMSS) were used to cover earnings in all industries at the national level.

Conceptual Differences

There are major differences in the coverage of earnings data among the three countries. In Canada, earnings data refer to all employees, including full-time and part-time employees. The employee concept excludes the owners or partners of unincorporated businesses and professional practices, the self-employed, and the unpaid family workers. The data refer to all industries (excluding agriculture, fishing, and trapping) in the private sector.

In the United States, earnings data are at the national level and include full-time wage and salary workers. In 1995, those workers accounted for 72 percent of total employment. Earnings by industry in the United States refer to production workers or nonsupervisory workers in private nonfarm industries. In 1995, those groups accounted for about four-fifths of total employment on private nonagriculture payrolls. Proprietors, the self-employed, and unpaid family workers were not included.

In Mexico, earnings data cover salary workers in the private formal sector (workers in enterprises that are registered with the IMSS). In 1995, the average number of enterprises registered at IMSS was 641,327, representing around 44 percent of total

wage and salary workers. In July 1993, IMSS's law was modified. Among the changes was a modification of the definition of basic earnings upon which contributions to the IMSS are made (*salario base de cotización*). The upper limit used to calculate basic earnings was revised upwards.[a] Data after 1993 are, therefore, not comparable with data from previous years.

In all three countries, employment data cover the same population as the earnings data.

Weekly earnings were converted to U.S. dollars using the prevailing market exchange rates. Although more useful for assessing relative competitiveness, market exchange rates are limited in comparing purchasing power. Thus, earnings were also converted to U.S. dollars using the purchasing power parities (PPPs) to eliminate the differences in prices levels among the countries. PPPs are given in national currency units per U.S. dollar.[b]

In all three countries, average weekly earnings include payments received by workers before payroll deductions such as premiums paid for overtime and benefits. In Canada, earnings data exclude employer contributions such as unemployment insurance, Canada/Quebec Pension Plans, provincial medical plans, worker's compensation, and other welfare plans. In Mexico, data exclude retirement insurance (SAR), housing contributions for workers (INFONAVIT), profit sharing, and savings funds equally contributed by workers and employers. In the United States, data exclude irregular bonuses and other special payments.

The minimum wage in Canada and the United States is set on an hourly basis. In contrast, in Mexico, it is set on a daily basis assuming an eight-hour day. In Mexico the Labor Law establishes that for each six days of work, workers will have a day of rest with full pay.

Labor income in all three countries is defined as payments received from wages, salaries, and supplementary income.

In Canada and the United States, supplementary labor income includes employer pension contributions; premiums for health insurance and other premium-based benefits; and payroll taxes for unemployment insurance, social assistance, worker's compensation, social security, and pensions. In Mexico, supplementary labor income refers to household monetary transfers, which includes payments received by households for social security, pensions, worker's compensation, premiums for injuries at work, and scholarships.

---

[a] Comisión Nacional de los Salarios Minimos, Campendio de Indicadores de Empleo y Salarios, December 1995.

[b] OECD. *National Accounts, Main Aggregates*, Vol. 1.

America, the median weekly earnings of skilled workers have increased more rapidly than the median earnings of unskilled workers, suggesting that this important factor influences income inequality. However, other factors such as experience gaps have to be taken into account.

Average Weekly Earnings and Inflation
in North America
As shown in Figure 53, the real average weekly earnings during 1984–1995 fluctuated more in Mexico than in Canada or the United States.

Figure 54 continues the analysis of North American earnings by showing the percentage of annual growth in each country by comparing current average weekly earnings and inflation during 1984–1995.

After a period of moderate decline, Canadian real average weekly earnings for all employees in the private sector began to recover in 1992. This situation was mainly a result of a significant reduc-

tion in the rate of inflation, and was also directly associated with an improvement in labor productivity (output per hour). By 1995 real earnings remained slightly (0.4 percent) below 1984 levels, while labor productivity in the business sector grew by 9.7 percent.

In Mexico, real average weekly earnings for wage and salary workers in the private formal sector decreased substantially during 1984–1988. By 1988, real earnings were 21 percent below 1984 levels. After 1989, as a result of a considerable reduction in inflation as well as an increase in labor productivity (output per employee), earnings began to recover, reaching higher levels in 1994 than in 1984. In 1995, a very strict monetary policy was implemented to stabilize the economy. Wages were increased at a moderate rate. This situation and the high rate of inflation pushed down real earnings once again. In 1995, real earnings dropped by 15 percent compared to the same period in 1994.

Figure 53

Real Average Weekly Earnings in North America 1984–1995

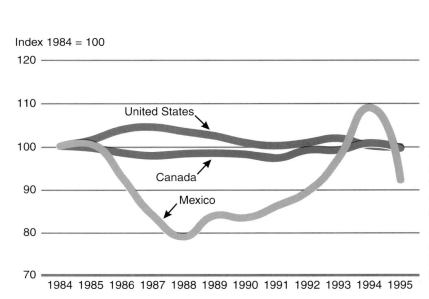

Index 1984 = 100

Note: National currency basis. For Canada, data are for all employees in the private sector, excluding workers in agriculture, fishing, and trapping. For Mexico, data are for wage and salary workers in the private formal sector. For the United States, data are median earnings for full-time wage and salary workers.

Source: Canada, Statistics Canada, Survey of Employment, Payroll, and Hours; Mexico, Mexian Institute of Social Security; United States, Bureau of Labor Statistics, Current Population Survey.

Figure 54

Current Average Weekly Earnings and Inflation in North America 1984–1995

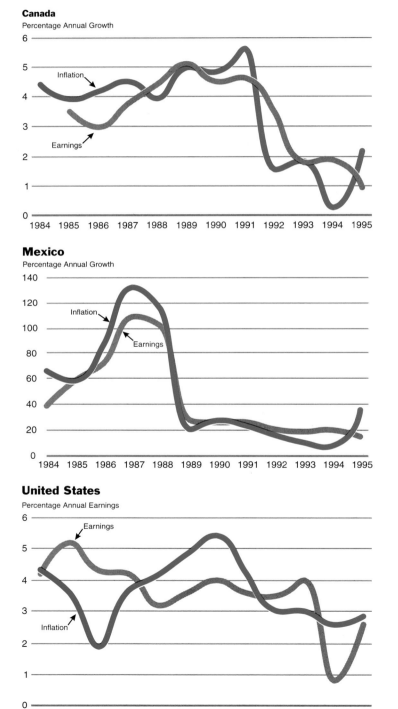

Canada
Percentage Annual Growth

Mexico
Percentage Annual Growth

United States
Percentage Annual Earnings

Note: National currency basis. For Canada, data are for employees in the private formal sector, excluding workers in agriculture, fishing, and trapping; Consumer Price Index 1986 = 100. For Mexico, data are for wage and salary workers in the private formal sector; Consumer Price Index 1994 = 100. For the United States, data are median earnings for full-time wage and salary workers; Consumer Price Index 1984 = 100.

Source: Canada, Statistics Canada, Survey of Employment, Payrolls, and Hours, and National Income and Expenditure Accounts; Mexico, Mexican Institute of Social Security and Bank of Mexico; United States, Bureau of Labor Statistics, Current Population Survey, and National Income and Product Accounts.

In the United States, real median weekly earnings of full-time wage and salary workers in the private sector increased during 1984–1988 by 3.6 percent. After 1988, real earnings declined. By 1995, the levels of real earning were the same as 1984 levels. In contrast, labor productivity (output per hour) in all private industries (business sector) increased by 11.8 percent between 1984 and 1995.

Total Average Weekly Earnings in U.S. Dollars in North America

Figure 55A and Figure 55B describe the trends of total weekly earnings in each North American country in U.S. dollars.

Until 1991, Canadian weekly earnings for all employees on a U.S. dollar basis increased, reducing the gap with the United States. This situation was mainly due to an increase in nominal earnings rather than changes in the exchange rate. By 1992, Canadian earnings began to decrease, but contrary to previous years, the main reason for the reduction was depreciation of the Canadian dollar relative to the U.S. dollar. As a result, the gap with U.S. earnings increased. By 1995, Canadian earnings were 13 percent below U.S. levels. Canadian earnings remained more than six times above Mexican levels. When purchasing power parities (PPPs) are used as the rate of currency conversion (see Figure 55B), Canadian earnings reduced their difference to 4 percent below U.S. levels in 1995. The difference between the Canadian and the Mexican earnings was reduced from a factor of six times to a factor of three times.

In Mexico, earnings for wage and salary workers in the private formal sector, in U.S. dollars, have remained below Canadian and U.S. levels during 1984–1995. In 1984, average weekly earnings in Mexico were 14.3 percent of U.S. levels and 15.2 percent of Canadian levels. In 1995, Mexican earnings relative to U.S. and Canadian levels decreased even further because of the devaluation of the peso in December 1994. Using PPPs, the difference between Mexican earnings in the private formal sector and earnings in Canada and the United States is reduced. In 1995, Mexican earn-

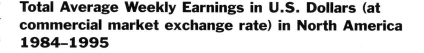

Figure 55A

Total Average Weekly Earnings in U.S. Dollars (at commercial market exchange rate) in North America 1984–1995

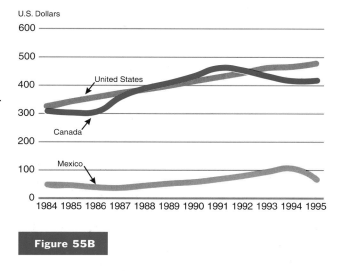

Figure 55B

Total Average Weekly Earnings in U.S. Dollars (at purchasing power parity) in North America 1984–1995

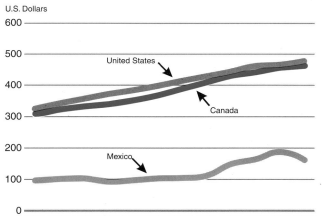

Note: In Figure 55A, the data was converted to U.S. dollars at commercial market exchange rates. In Figure 55B, the data was converted to U.S. dollars using purchasing power parity (PPPs). For Canada, data are for all employees in the private sector, excluding workers in agriculture, fishing, and trapping. For Mexico, data are for wage and salary workers in the formal private sector. For the United States, data are median earnings for full-time wage and salary workers.

Source: Canada, Statistics Canada, Survey of Employment, Payrolls, and Hours; Mexico, Mexican Institute of Social Security; United States, Bureau of Labor Statistics, Current Population Survey.

Figure 56

Employment and Real Average Weekly Earnings in North America 1984–1994

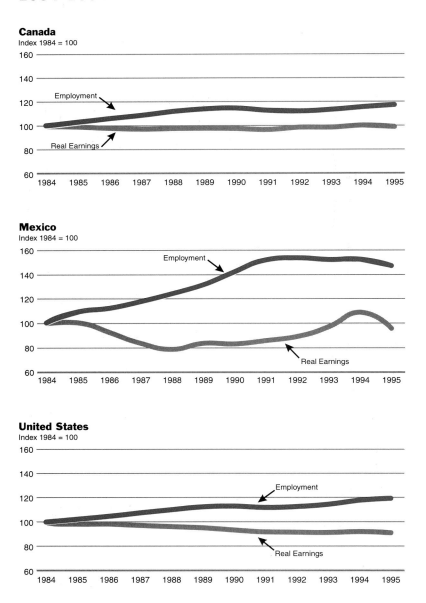

Canada
Index 1984 = 100

Mexico
Index 1984 = 100

United States
Index 1984 = 100

Note: For Canada, data are for all employees in the private sector, excluding workers in agriculture, fishing, and trapping. For Mexico, data are for wage and salary workers in the private formal sector. For the United States, data are median earnings for full-time wage and salary workers.

Source: Canada, Statistics Canada, Survey of Employment, Payrolls, and Hours; Mexico, Mexican Institute of Social Security; United States, Bureau of Labor Statistics, Current Population Survey.

ings using commercial market exchange rates represented 13 percent of U.S. levels, while the ratio increased to 34 percent using PPPs. In comparison to Canadian levels, the ratio increased from 15 percent to 35 percent in the same year.

Between 1984 and 1995, the United States had the highest average weekly earnings on a U.S. dollar basis among North American countries. U.S nominal average weekly earnings for full-time wage and salary workers in the private formal sector during 1984–1995 increased by 49 percent, while Canadian and Mexican earnings in terms of U.S. dollars (at commercial market exchange rate) increased at lower rates (35 percent and 39 percent, respectively). As a result, the earnings gap among the three countries increased. When PPPs are used as the rate of currency conversion, the earnings gap is reduced.

Employment and Real Average Weekly Earnings in North America

In general during 1984–1995, employment growth in North American countries occurred in the context of a decline in real earnings in the Mexican private formal sector and in real earnings stagnation in Canada and the United States (see Figure 56).

In Canada, employment levels (excluding agriculture, fishing, and trapping) in 1995 were 16.8 percent higher than 1984 levels, while real average earnings remained almost constant with a small reduction of only 0.4 percent. Between 1984 and 1990 employment growth was strong while real earnings decreased. After a two-year decline because of economic recession, employment recovered its rate of growth in 1993. At the same time, earnings growth recovered.

In Mexico, formal employment in the private sector (measured by the number of insured workers at the Mexican Institute of Social Security) between 1984 and 1991 grew at a high rate (6.8 percent annually), while real earnings were substantially reduced. In 1991, employment was 51 percent higher than 1984 levels. In contrast, real earnings had declined by 14 percent. From 1991 to 1994, employment in the formal sector continued increasing, but at a lower rate than in previous years; meanwhile, earnings recovered. In 1995, the economic contraction reduced employment levels by 2.9 percent in comparison to 1994, and real earnings were significantly reduced by 15.0 percent as a result of a moderation in wage adjustments and a high increase in the inflation rate.

In the United States, employment growth in the private sector between 1984 and 1988 occurred in the context of an increase in real average weekly earnings. From 1988, earnings declined while employment continued growing. In 1995, employment levels of wage and salary workers were 19 percent above the 1984 levels, while real earnings levels of those workers remained unchanged.

Labor Income in North America and Supplementary Labor Income in Canada and the United States
Labor income (which includes wages, salaries, and supplementary income) as a proportion of GDP increased in Canada up to 1994, but did not change in the United States or in Mexico (see Figure 57A). Employees in all three countries have been receiving a greater share of their labor income in the form of supplementary income.

In Canada, the share of labor income in GDP increased from 58 percent in 1984 to 61 percent in 1994. This situation was mainly the result of a higher rate of growth in supplementary income (8.5 percent per annum) compared to wage and salary growth (5.6 percent per annum). As a result, the proportion of supplementary income in the GDP rose by 1.8 percentage points, while the share of wages and salaries increased by 1.1 percentage points (see Figure 57B).

In Mexico, the share of labor income in the GDP remained almost constant, accounting for 29.0 percent in 1994. This figure includes only income received by wage and salary workers, which accounted for 59.0 percent of total employment in 1995.[2] Benefits have increased as a proportion of total income in Mexico. According to

Labor Income in North America 1984–1995

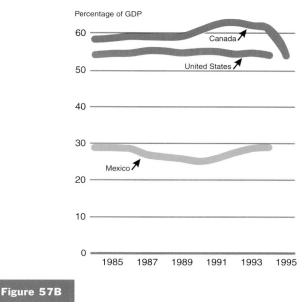

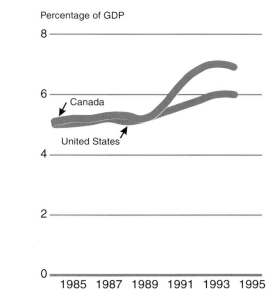

Canada and the United States: Supplementary Labor Income 1984–1995

Note: The data represent wage and salary workers for Mexico.

Source: Canada, Statistics Canada, National Income and Expenditure Accounts; Mexico, INEGI, System of National Accounts; United States, Bureau of the Census, National Income and Product Accounts.

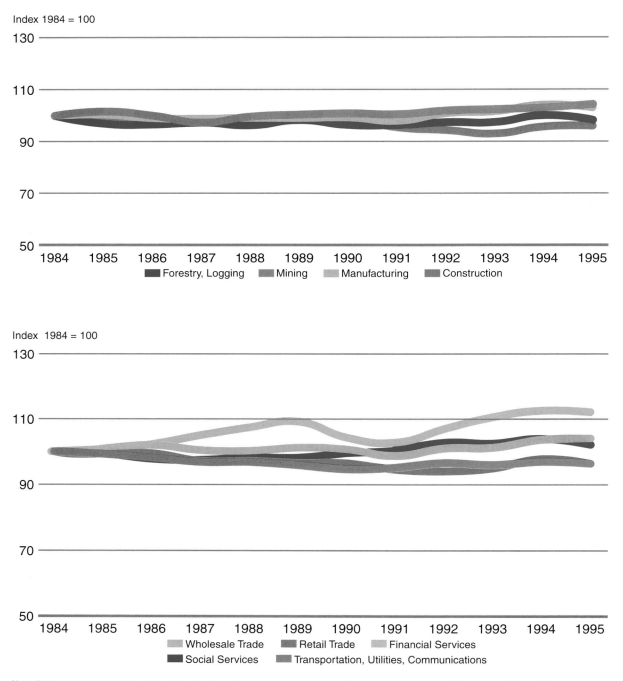

Figure 58

Canada: Real Average Weekly Earnings Growth by Sector 1984–1995

Note: National currency basis. Data refer to all employees. Earnings were deflated by the Consumer Price Index 1984 = 100.

Source: Statistics Canada, Bureau of Employment, Payrolls, and Hours.

the National Expenditure and Income Survey, benefits as a proportion of total household income increased from 6.2 percent in 1984 to 7.6 percent in 1994. The Industrial Monthly Survey reported that between 1987 and 1995 benefits in the manufacturing sector increased at a higher rate (3.2 percent per annum) than wages and salaries (2.3 percent per annum). As a result, the share of benefits in the total income increased from 28.7 percent to 30.9 percent in the same period.

In the United States, the share of labor income in the GDP remained virtually constant over the period. Nonetheless, supplementary income grew at an annual rate of 7.8 percent in 1984–1994, and wages and salaries grew at 5.7 percent annually. As a result, the share of supplementary income in the GDP increased by 1.0 percentage point between 1984 and 1994, while the share of wages and salaries decreased by 1.0 percentage point (see Figure 57B).

Canada: Real Average Weekly Earnings Growth by Sector

There is significant dispersion in average weekly earnings among sectors in the three North America countries. During 1984–1995, none of these countries experienced substantial changes in this respect. The following discussion of weekly earnings will begin with Canada (see Figures 58 and 59).

As shown in Figure 58, earnings differences among sectors in Canada did not change substantially between 1984 and 1994. The main change was the increase in real earnings in the financial and real estate sector, which rose 12 percent during the period. This sector also had the highest rate of employment growth over the period. In other sectors with high employment growth rates (such as retail trade and social services), earnings did not show an improvement. In retail trade, earnings declined throughout the period, while in social

Figure 59

Canada: Real Average Weekly Earnings by Sector
1984 and 1995

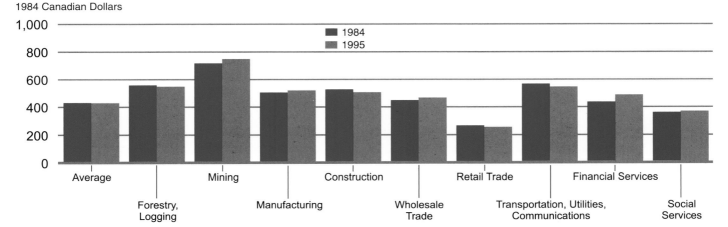

1984 Canadian Dollars

Note: Data refer to all employees in the private sector, excluding workers in agriculture, fishing, and trapping.

Source: Statistics Canada, Survey of Employment, Payrolls, and Hours.

Figure 60

Mexico: Real Average Weekly Earnings Growth by Sector 1984–1995

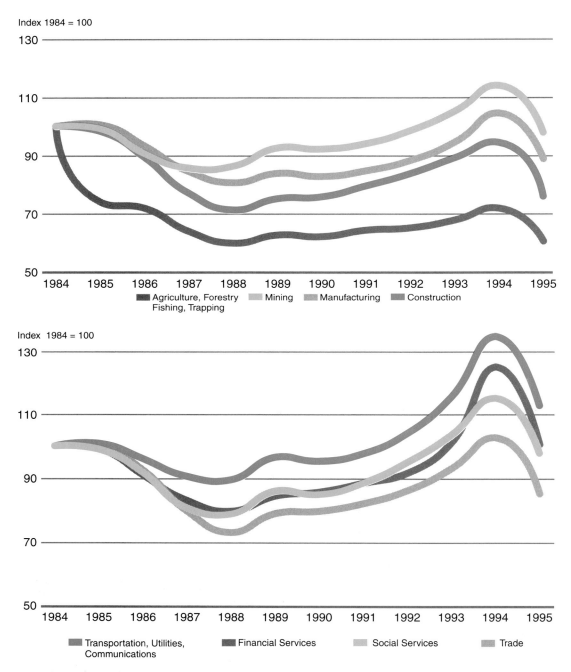

Index 1984 = 100

Agriculture, Forestry Fishing, Trapping ■ Mining ■ Manufacturing ■ Construction

Index 1984 = 100

■ Transportation, Utilities, Communications ■ Financial Services ■ Social Services ■ Trade

Note: National currency basis. Data refer to workers in the formal private sector. Earnings were deflated by the Consumer Price Index 1994 = 100.

Source: Mexico, Mexican Institute of Social Security.

services, although earnings increased slightly, levels remained below the national average.

Canada: Real Average Weekly Earnings by Sector
Workers in the mining sector of Canada had the highest real average weekly earnings (see Figure 59). In 1995, average earnings in this sector were 74.0 percent above the national average. In contrast, the lowest earnings were in retail trade and social services with levels 40.0 percent and 14.0 percent below the national average, respectively. These sectors absorbed almost 44.0 percent of total employment in 1995, while mining was only 1.2 percent of total employment in the same year. In the manufacturing sector, real earnings were 21.0 percent above the national average. In comparison to other industries, average earnings in the manufacturing sector were the fourth highest.

Mexico: Real Average Weekly Earnings Growth by Sector
As shown in Figure 60, all economic sectors in Mexico experienced reductions in real earnings

between 1984 and 1988. However, from 1989 to 1994 there was a substantial recovery. The highest increases were in transportation, communications, and financial services. This last sector has been one of the most important employment absorbers in the private formal sector in Mexico. In contrast, earnings in the primary, trade, and construction sectors, which are lower than the national average, did not rise enough by 1994 to reach their 1984 levels.

Although real earnings in the social services sector increased substantially over this period, levels were still 10 percent below the national average in 1994. In the manufacturing sector, where employment growth has slowed (except in the *maquiladora* industry), earnings have remained slightly below the national average.

Mexico: Real Average Weekly Earnings by Sector
Real earnings for wage and salary workers in the private formal sector of Mexico were highest in transportation, communications, and financial services sectors. In 1995, the average earnings in these

Figure 61

Mexico: Real Average Weekly Earnings by Sector 1984 and 1995

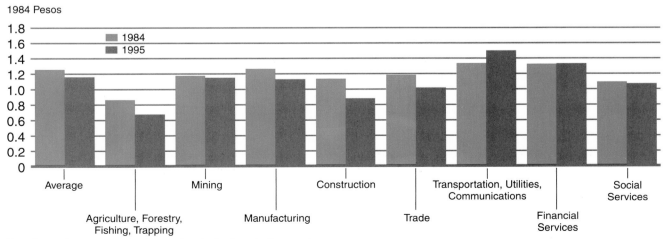

1984 Pesos

Note: Data refer to wage and salary workers in the formal private sector.

Source: Mexico, Mexican Institute of Social Security.

89

Figure 62

United States: Real Average Weekly Earnings Growth by Sector 1984–1995

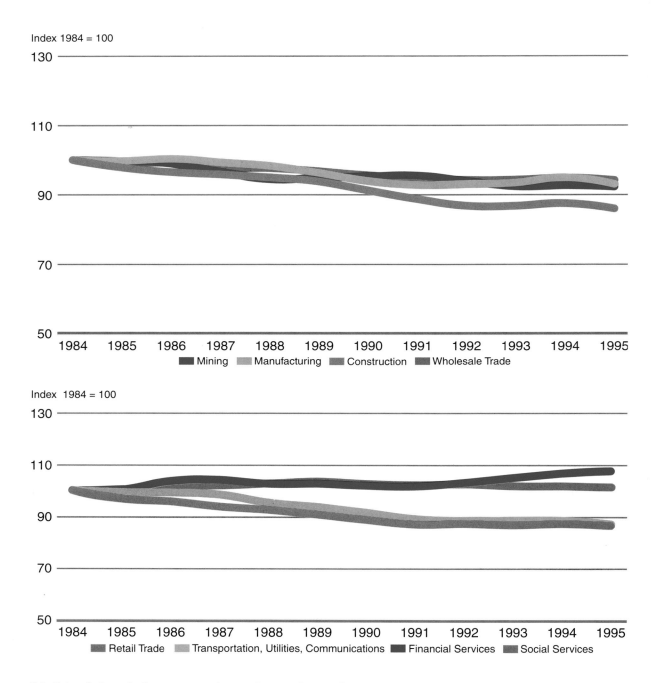

Index 1984 = 100

Mining — Manufacturing — Construction — Wholesale Trade

Index 1984 = 100

Retail Trade — Transportation, Utilities, Communications — Financial Services — Social Services

Note: Data refer to production or nonsupervisory workers on private nonfarm payrolls. Earnings were deflated by the Consumer Price Index 1982–1984 = 100.

Source: United States, Bureau of Census, Current Employment Statistics Survey.

two sectors were 29 percent and 15 percent above the national average, respectively (see Figure 61). The lowest earnings were in the primary sector, construction, trade, and social services, which were more than 10 percent lower than the average. These latter sectors accounted for 33 percent of total insured workers in 1995.

United States: Real Average Weekly Earnings Growth by Sector

Figure 62 shows that in the United States, most sectors have experienced a declining trend in real average earnings of production or nonsupervisory workers between 1984 and 1995, with the exception of financial and social services. (Note that including relatively well-paid supervisory workers in these data might have changed this trend.) The largest reductions occurred in the retail trade,

construction, and transportation sectors. In the service sector, real average earnings improved slightly, with the greatest increase in earnings in financial services. The service and financial sectors experienced the highest rate of employment growth in the same period.

United States: Real Average Weekly Earnings by Sector

In the United States, the highest average earnings of nonsupervisory production workers in nonfarm industries were in the mining, construction, and transportation sectors, whose levels in 1995 were more than 40.0 percent above the average for the total private sector (see Figure 63). The lowest levels were in the retail trade and social services sectors with earnings 44.0 percent and 6.4 percent, respectively, below the national average. In the manufac-

Figure 63

United States: Real Average Weekly Earnings by Sector 1984 and 1995

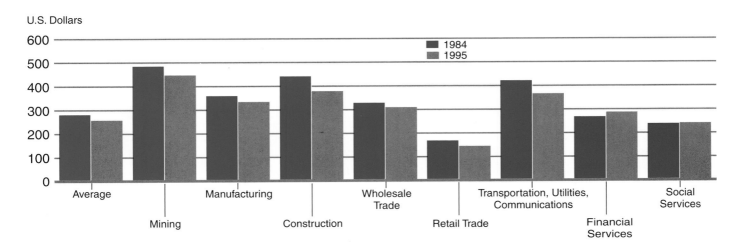

U.S. Dollars

Note: Data refer to production or nonsupervisory workers on private nonfarm payrolls.

Source: United States, Bureau of Census, Current Employment Statistics Survey.

Table 2A

Dispersion of Median Weekly Earnings by Education Level in Canada and the United States

Canada[a]	1984	1994
0 to 8 years		
Male	59	57
Female	47	46
High school graduates		
Male	64	67
Female	59	62
Some post-secondary school		
Male	71	68
Female	64	64
Post-secondary certificate or diploma		
Male	74	76
Female	72	68

United States[b]	1984	1995
Less than a high school diploma	58	45
High school graduates, no college	71	63
Some college or associate degree	84	74

Note: Weekly earnings dispersion in Canada and the United States is measured as the ratio of each educational earnings level to the upper educational earning level of a university degree for Canada and a bachelor's degree for the United States.

[a] For Canada data cover full-time workers. Graduates from high school in 1984 include only some high school.

[b] In the United States data cover full-time wage and salary workers who are 25 years and over. Educational attainment data since 1992 have been based on the highest diploma or degree received rather than the number of years of school completed. Thus, data for 1995 are not directly comparable with 1984 data.

[c] Data for Mexico refer to the share of workers by multiples of the minimum wage according to the levels of education of each minimum-wage group. Data cover all workers.

Source: Canada, Statistics Canada, Household Survey Division, Income Labour, Expenditure, and Housing Data; Mexico, STPSS/INEGI, National Employment Survey; United States, Bureau of Labor Statistics, U.S. Current Population Survey.

Table 2B

Employment Distribution by Multiple of Minimum Wage and Levels of Education in Mexico[c]

	1991			1995		
	≤2	2.01 to 5	5+	≤2	2.01 to 5	5+
Six years or fewer	65	40	23	61	35	18
Less than high school	19	18	13	23	21	11
High school	12	23	17	12	24	18
Some college or associate degree	4	19	47	4	19	53

turing sector, although earnings of production workers declined, levels remained almost 30.0 percent above average private sector earnings in 1995.

Earnings and Educations Levels

In all three countries, workers with higher levels of education have higher levels of earnings, and the earnings income gap between men and women is reduced as levels of education increase (see Table 2A).

In Canada in 1994, the median earnings for full-time male workers with eight years of education or less was 43 percent less of the median earnings for men with a university degree; for women the earnings ratio was 54 percent. The earnings gap between men and women is also reduced at higher levels of education: in 1994, the ratio of female earnings to male earnings for those with eight years of education or less was 64 percent, while the earnings ratio of female to male workers with university degrees increased to 79 percent.

As Table 2B indicates, in 1995, 61 percent of Mexican workers earning less than two times the minimum wage had a sixth grade education or less; 64 percent of workers who earned between two and five times the minimum wage had at least a secondary level of education; 82 percent of employees with high school or higher had incomes above five times the minimum wage. These proportions, compared with those observed in 1991, suggest that earnings increased for more-educated workers (more than high school), while earnings were reduced for less-educated workers (high school or less).

In the United States, full-time wage and salary workers with higher average weekly earnings had higher educational levels.[3] In 1995, the median earnings for workers with less than a high school diploma were 55 percent less than the level of earnings for workers with advanced degrees. The earnings gap between women and men is reduced as women's educational levels increase. Generally, the median earnings of women with less than a high school diploma were 24 percent less than the median earnings for men with the same level of

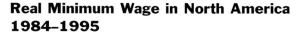

Real Minimum Wage in North America 1984–1995

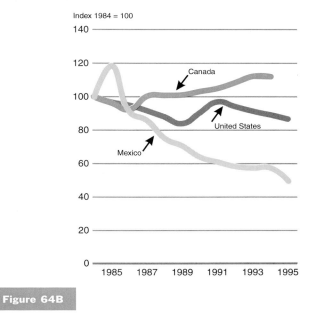

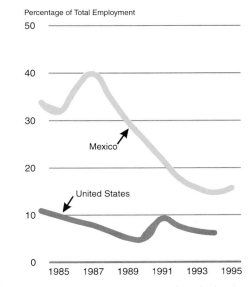

Mexico and the United States: Minimum Wage Workers 1984–1995

Note: For Mexico, minimum wage workers were in the formal private sector.

Source: Canada, Statistics Canada and Human Resources Development Canada; Mexico, National Commission for Minimum Wages; United States, Bureau of Labor Statistics, Current Population Survey.

education, while it was 15 percent less for women with advanced degrees.

The median weekly earnings of skilled workers in the United States and Canada have increased at a higher rate than those of unskilled workers. In the United States during 1984–1991, the earnings of workers with less than four years of high school rose at an annual rate of 2.3 percent, while earnings of workers with four years of college or more grew twice as fast (4.6 percent per annum). Between 1992 and 1995 this situation persisted. In Canada, median earnings for male and female workers with a university degree increased by 35.0 percent and

50.0 percent, respectively, during 1984–1994; whereas male and female workers with eight years of education or less saw smaller increases in their median earnings of 30.0 percent and 47.0 percent, respectively.

Real Minimum Wage in North America and Minimum Wage Workers in Mexico and the United States

As shown in Figure 64A, the real minimum wage in Mexico and the United States declined substantially between 1984 and 1995, while it increased in Canada. In 1995, the minimum wage was 51 per-

DATA ISSUES:

Compensation, Productivity, and Unit Labor Costs

Sources of Information

For Canada, the data used in the analysis were taken from "Aggregate Productivity Measures 1993" published by Statistics Canada and from information provided directly by this institution. Statistics Canada derives data from several sources. GDP data for the manufacturing sector were at constant prices and came from the National Income and Expenditure Accounts. The number of hours worked was obtained from the annual Survey of Manufacturers.

For Mexico, data came from the Monthly Industrial Survey (MIS) that is conducted by INEGI. Up to 1987, this survey covered 1,157 establishments. In 1988, the sample was increased to 3,218 establishments. This survey excludes self-employed and unpaid workers. It covers 129 industries in large establishments (with more than six workers and revenues of 3 million pesos or more) that represent more than 70 percent of manufacturing GDP. The data came from "Indicadores de Competitividad de la Economía Mexicana" prepared by INEGI.

For the United States, the data used were those published by the Bureau of Labor Statistics in "International Comparisons of Manufacturing Productivity and Unit Labor Costs Trends, 1995."[a] Compensation data were derived from the Employment Cost Index (ECI) Survey. Labor productivity (output per hour) data were

derived from several sources: GDP from the National Income and Product Accounts and hours worked from the Current Employment Statistics (CES) Program, and from the Current Population Survey.

Conceptual Differences

Hourly compensation costs are defined as compensation costs per employee hour worked. Hourly compensation costs for manufacturing production workers include all payments made directly to the worker for time worked and for time not worked, bonuses and other special payments, and employer expenditures for legally required insurance programs and for contractual and private benefit plans. In Mexico, costs do not include payments made by employers for retirement insurance (SAR). In Canada and the United States, costs include employed workers and self-employed workers in the production process. In Mexico, costs include employees in production and administration, and exclude self-employed workers.

Compensation costs were converted to U.S. dollars using the prevailing market exchange rates, which are more useful for assessing relative competitiveness.

In all three countries, labor productivity refers to output per hour worked. Although labor input is an important determinant in the level of output, it is not the only one. Other inputs (such as cent below the 1984 level in Mexico, and 13 percent below its 1984 level in the United States. However, in both countries the percentage of minimum-wage workers was considerably reduced throughout the period (see Figure 64B). In Canada, the minimum wage in real terms decreased in 1984 and 1985. Afterwards, it recovered growth, increasing by 12 percent in 1994 compared to the 1984 level. In 1986, it was estimated that 9 percent of all paid workers had earnings at or below the minimum wage in Canada.[4]

In 1995, the federal minimum wage in the United States was $4.25 per hour. Some states had

capital, materials, and services) contribute to the production process. In all three countries, labor productivity is constructed as a ratio of real manufacturing output index to the hours worked index. For Canada and the United States, the output measure refers to value added, while in Mexico it refers to the gross value of production. In Canada and the United States, data refer to all employed persons (employees and self-employed workers), while in Mexico data exclude self-employed workers.

Unit labor cost is the ratio of labor compensation to real GDP. It is a measure of the cost of labor per unit of real output. Unit labor cost can be viewed as the ratio of average compensation to labor productivity. Thus, unit labor costs will increase when average compensation grows more rapidly than labor productivity.

In Canada and the United States, unit labor costs cover all manufacturing industries, while in Mexico those costs refer to 129 manufacturing industries, which account for around 70 percent of total manufacturing GDP.

a U.S. Department of Labor, "News," July 17, 1996.

higher minimums, with the highest levels in Hawaii and the District of Columbia at $5.25 per hour. In Mexico, the minimum wage is fixed on a daily basis with an eight-hour day as the norm. In 1995, the national average minimum wage was 16.4 new pesos per day (less than U.S.$3.00 per day).[5] There are three distinct levels of minimum wage, applicable to different geographic areas, and minimum occupational salaries for 88 occupations that are higher than the basic minimum.[6] In Canada, the minimum wage is set at the provincial level, with an average of $5.80 per hour in 1995. The average for Ontario, Quebec, and British Columbia, the three largest provinces, is $6.75 per hour (approximately U.S.$5.00 per hour).

In all three countries, minimum-wage employment is higher among women. In Canada, women accounted for 60.0 percent of those earning the minimum wage or less in 1986. In the United States, 7.8 percent of total female employment in 1994 earned the minimum wage while the share for men was 4.7 percent. In Mexico, 23.6 percent of women workers earned the minimum wage or less in 1995, compared to 16.9 percent of male workers. Although in Mexico and in the United States the proportion of men and women earning the minimum wage has decreased, the women's proportion has fallen more rapidly in both countries. This situation suggests that there has been a reduction in the salary gap between men and women at low income levels.

Trends in Productivity: Hourly Compensation Costs, Labor Productivity, and Unit Labor Costs in Manufacturing

Overview

Although manufacturing employment in the three countries has reduced its share in total employment, it still remains one of the major sources of employment in North American countries. The three countries experienced an increasing trend in hourly manufacturing compensation costs in terms of U.S. dollars during most of 1984–1994. In general, the United States had the highest hourly compensation costs, while Mexico had the lowest.

All three countries increased their labor productivity (output per hour worked) in the manufacturing sector during 1984 and 1995. During 1993–1995, labor productivity increased substantially, growing at a higher rate than compensation costs. As a result, unit labor costs in the manufacturing sector have been reduced.

Hourly Compensation Costs in Manufacturing in North America

Figure 65 shows that Canadian compensation costs in the manufacturing sector in terms of U.S. dollars increased at a higher rate than U.S. compensation costs during 1984–1995. As a result, Canadian levels reduced the difference from U.S.

levels from 11 percent in 1984 to 7 percent in 1995. During 1993–1995, manufacturing costs fell relative to U.S. levels, mainly because of the depreciation of the Canadian dollar.

In Mexico, manufacturing compensation costs in terms of U.S. dollars had the fastest growth rate during 1987–1994. The devaluation of the peso at the end of 1994 brought a drastic reduction of manufacturing costs in 1995, which declined by 40 percent from 1993. In 1995, Mexican compensation costs per hour worked in the manufacturing sector represented about 19 percent of U.S. levels and 20 percent of Canadian levels.

In the United States, compensation costs per hour worked in the manufacturing sector increased throughout 1984–1995, remaining above the Canadian and Mexican levels for most of the period. Since 1992, compensation cost growth has observed a declining trend.

Labor Productivity, Hourly Labor Compensation, and Unit Labor Costs Growth in Manufacturing in North America

Labor productivity (output per hour worked) in the manufacturing sector in North American countries increased during 1984–1995 (see Figures 66 and 67).

During 1984–1991, labor productivity in the Canadian manufacturing sector grew at a lower rate (0.8 percent annually) than hourly compensation costs (4.6 percent). As a result, unit labor costs increased at a high rate (3.8 percent). Between 1991 and 1995, labor productivity increased substantially (2.8 percent per annum). When combined with a lower compensation cost growth (1.6 percent annually), this change resulted in a significant reduction in unit labor costs. The growth in productivity between 1991 and 1995 was basically explained by a manufacturing output increase of 4.4 percent per annum, since hours worked grew at 1.6 percent.

During 1986–1994, labor productivity in large manufacturing establishments in Mexico grew at a rate of 6.3 percent annually. This performance in labor productivity combined with a lower growth

Figure 65

Hourly Compensation Costs in Manufacturing in North America 1984–1995

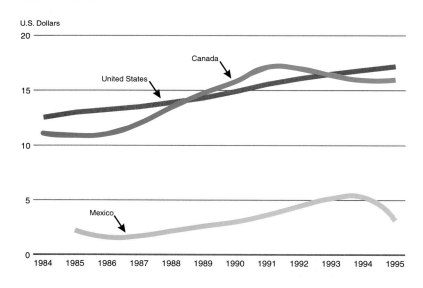

Note: Converted to U.S. dollars at commercial market exchange rates.

Source: Canada, Statistics Canada, Survey of Employment, Payrolls, and Hours; Mexico, INEGI, Industrial Monthly Survey; United States, Bureau of Census, Current Employment Statistics Survey.

Figure 66

Labor Productivity, Hourly Labor Compensation, and Unit Labor Costs Growth in Manufacturing in North America

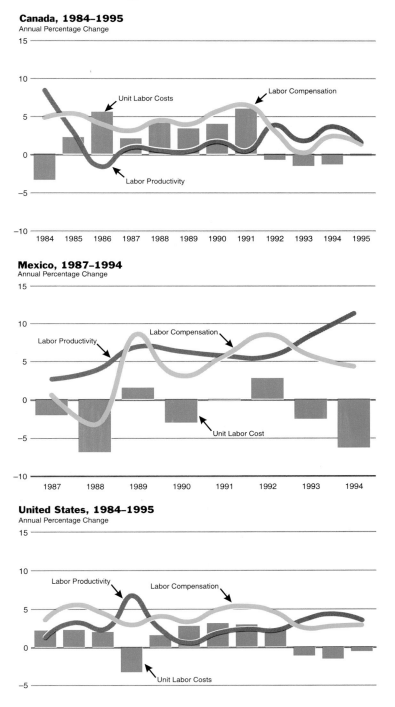

Canada, 1984–1995
Annual Percentage Change

Mexico, 1987–1994
Annual Percentage Change

United States, 1984–1995
Annual Percentage Change

Note: National currency basis. The labor productivity measure is output per hour worked.

Source: Canada, Statistics Canada, Survey of Employment, Payrolls, and Hours, and National Income and Expenditure Accounts; Mexico, INEGI, Monthly Industrial Survey; United States, Bureau of Labor Statistics, Current Employment Statistics Program, and National Income and Product Accounts.

Output and Hours Worked Growth in Manufacturing in North America

Canada, 1984–1995
Annual Percentage Growth

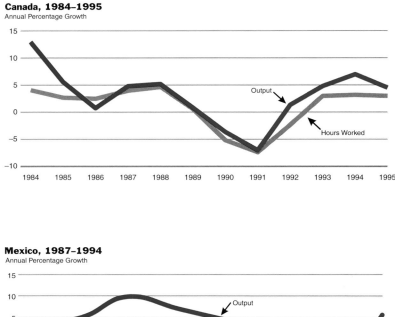

Mexico, 1987–1994
Annual Percentage Growth

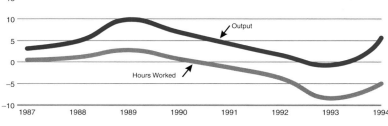

United States, 1984–1995
Annual Percentage Growth

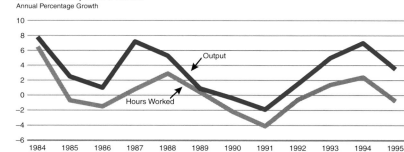

Source: Canada, Statistics Canada, Annual Survey of Manufacturers and Income and Expenditures; Mexico, INEGI, Industrial Monthly Survey; United States, Department of Labor, Bureau of Labor Statistics.

in compensation cost (4.0 percent annually) resulted in a substantial reduction in unit labor costs, which declined by 2.3 percent annually during 1986–1994. The growth in manufacturing labor productivity in Mexico during this period was explained mainly by a manufacturing output increase of 4.5 percent annually combined with a reduction of hours worked of 1.8 percent annually.

In the United States, manufacturing labor productivity grew at a moderate rate between 1984 and 1991, averaging 2.7 percent annually. From 1991, productivity in the manufacturing sector had a substantial increase, growing at an annual rate of 3.4 percent during 1991–1995. This performance was a result of an output manufacturing increase of 4.2 percent per year combined with a 0.8 percent growth in hours worked. As labor productivity increased at a higher rate than hourly compensation costs, unit labor costs in the manufacturing sector were reduced by 1.1 percent during 1991–1995.

Trends in Income Distribution

Overview

During 1984–1995, income inequality after taxes and after transfers has increased in Mexico and in the United States, and it has dropped slightly in Canada, although overall more households were moving toward higher levels of income. Income depends on various factors such as wage rates, work attachment, and household composition and size. In Mexico, the rise in the number of earners per household is one of the main factors explaining household income growth. In Canada and the United States, the average numbers of earners per household has remained almost constant over the period.

In Canada, real average income of family and unattached individuals after taxes and after transfers remained almost unchanged during 1984–1993, while in Mexico and the United States it increased during 1984–1994. In these last two

Figure 68

Share of Aggregate Household Income by Quintile in North America 1984 and 1994

Canada

Percentage of Income

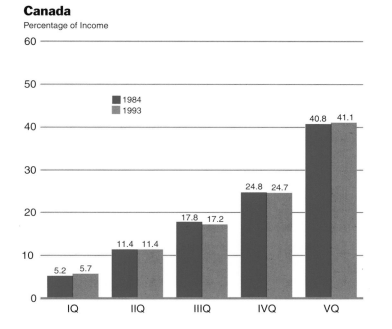

■ 1984
■ 1993

Note: Through 1993 for Canada. Canadian data refer to family and unattached individual income. Data are after taxes and after transfers in all three countries.

Source: Canada, Statistics Canada, Survey of Consumer Finances; Mexico, INEGI, National Income and Expenditure Survey; United States, Bureau of the Census, Current Population Survey.

Mexico

Percentage of Income

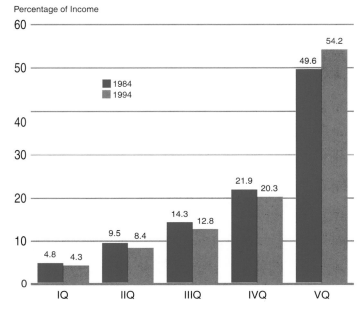

■ 1984
■ 1994

United States

Percentage of Income

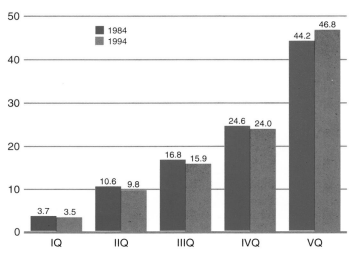

■ 1984
■ 1994

countries, the major increases in income went to the top household quintile (highest 20 percent). Thus, the income gap between the top quintile and the other four quintiles of households grew in the United States and Mexico. In Canada, the income gap between the top quintile and the lowest quintile was reduced, while it increased between the top and the next three quintiles. In the United States and Canada, taxation policy and government trans-

fers had a positive impact on reducing income differences among households (families and unattached individuals).

Share of Aggregate Household Income by Quintile in North America
As shown in Figure 68, the top 20 percent of all families and unattached individuals in Canada received 41 percent of total income (after taxes and

DATA ISSUES:

Income Distribution

Sources of Information

Mexican income distribution data came from the National Income and Expenditure Survey (ENIGH) carried out on a periodic basis by INEGI. The ENIGH survey was first conducted in 1984. Since then there have been three more surveys: 1989, 1992, and 1994. Data from these surveys are comparable, since there have been no major conceptual changes. The survey sample represents all private households.

The information for Canada came from the Survey of Consumer Finances (SCF) conducted annually by Statistics Canada since 1971. The SCF uses a sample representing virtually all private households and individuals in Canada.

For the United States, income information came from the Current Population Survey (CPS). As a result of the redesign of this survey in 1994 and the implementation of 1990 census population controls, income data for 1994 and 1995 are not strictly comparable with early years. Income refers to money before taxes and excludes capital gains. Estimations of tax data are prepared by the Housing and Household Economic and Statistics Division and are based on modeled data.[a]

Conceptual Differences—Income

In all three countries, the concept of income used in the analysis of income distribution includes wages and salaries, net income

from self-employment, investment income, government transfer payments, and miscellaneous income. There are differences not only in the items included in government transfer payments, but also in the amount received from those payments among the countries. One of the major definitional differences is that in Canada and the United States, income refers to monetary income, while in Mexico it refers to monetary and nonmonetary income. In 1994, almost three-quarters of total household income in Mexico was monetary income.

The concept of income used in the analysis refers to disposable income, defined as income after taxes and transfers, unless otherwise indicated.

Conceptual Differences—Income Distribution

Income distribution data for the United States and Mexico are based on households, while data for Canada are based on families and unattached individuals. An unattached individual is defined as a person living alone or in a household where he or she is not related to other household members. Another difference is that in the United States and Canada, income refers to the income received in the preceding calendar year; in Mexico, it refers to the income received in the previous reference month.

The concept of government transfers in all three countries refers to cash payments. In Canada, it includes all social welfare payments from federal, provincial, and municipal governments includes transfers) in 1993. Inequality of income is evident in the differences of average income of families and unattached individuals per quintiles. In the same year, the ratio of the average income of the lowest quintile to the highest quintile was 1:7.3.

In Mexico, the top 20 percent of all households received 54.2 percent of the aggregate income (after taxes and includes transfers) in 1994. In the

such as child tax benefits, old age security, guaranteed income supplements, spousal allowances, Canada and Quebec Pension Plan benefits, unemployment insurance benefits, and worker's compensation. In the United States, transfers include public assistance, unemployment insurance, social security, workers' compensation, retirement income, and education funds. Excluded are noncash transfers such as Medicare, school lunches, Medicaid, and other means-tested government noncash transfers. In Mexico, transfers include monetary payments received from social security programs such as medical care, disability, old age, dismissal at an advanced age, death, and worker's compensation benefits.

The Gini coefficient is a summary measure of income inequality. It ranges from 0.0 when every household (family and unattached individual) has the same income, to 1.0 when one household (family and unattached individual) has all the income.

a U.S. Department of Commerce, Bureau of the Census, "Money Income in the United States: 1995," *Current Population Reports*, September 1996.

Figure 69

Canada and the United States: Share of Aggregate Household Income Before and After Taxes and Transfers by Quintile
1994

Canada
Percentage of Income

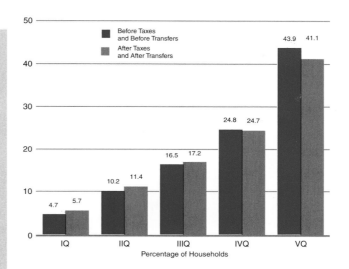

Percentage of Households

United States
Percentage of Income

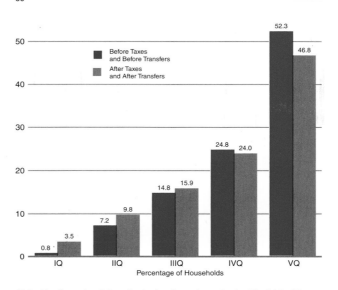

Percentage of Households

Note: For Canada, data refer to family and unattached individual income.

Source: Canada, Statistics Canada, Survey of Consumer Finances; United States, Bureau of the Census, Current Population Survey.

Figure 70

Household Gini Coefficient After Taxes and After Transfers in North America 1984–1994

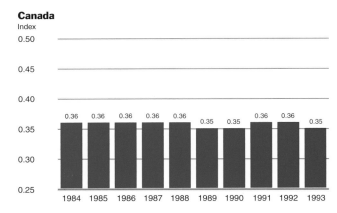

Canada
Index

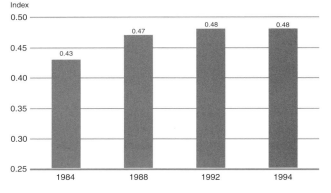

Mexico
Index

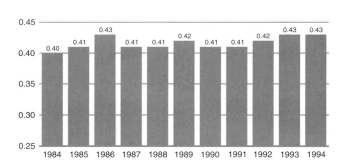

United States
Index

Note: For Canada, data refer to family and unattached individual income. For Mexico and the United States, data are for households.

Source: Canada, Statistics Canada, Survey of Consumer Finances; Mexico, INEGI, National Income and Expenditure Survey; United States, Bureau of the Census, Current Population Survey.

same year, the ratio of the average income of the lowest quintile to the highest quintile was 1:13.

In the United States, the top 20 percent of households accounted for almost 47 percent of total income in 1994. In the same year, the ratio of the average income after taxes and after transfers of the lowest quintile to the highest quintile was 1:13.

Canada and United States: Share of Aggregate Household Income Before and After Taxes by Quintile

In the United States and Canada (see Figure 69), taxation policy and government transfers had a positive impact on reducing income differences among households (families and unattached individuals). Comparing income distribution before taxes and before transfers to income distribution after taxes and after transfers shows that in both countries, the first three quintiles increased their share of total income, while the income share of the highest quintile decreased. This situation is also evident in the change of the Gini coefficient and indicates a reduction of inequality in income distribution when both taxes and transfers are considered.

In Canada, the Gini coefficient was reduced by 30 percent for Canadian families and unattached individuals in 1993, and by 15.6 percent for United States households in 1994. In both Canada and the United States government transfers have a greater impact on lowering income inequality than the tax system. In the United States, including taxes from the calculation lowered the Gini coefficient by 4.5 percent in 1994, while including transfers reduced the Gini coefficient by 11.0 percent. In Canada, the Gini coefficient is reduced by 9.5 percent when considering taxes and by 22.0 percent when considering transfers.

Household Gini Coefficient After Taxes and After Transfers in North America

Figure 70 gives another way to examine household income in North America: by Gini coefficient after taxes and after transfers. For Canada, the evolution of the Gini coefficient indicates that the distribution of income improved slightly during

Figure 71

Distribution of Households by Income Group in North America

Canada
1984 and 1993
Percentage of Families and Individuals

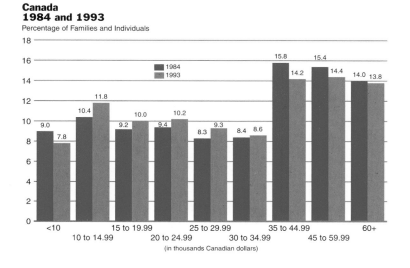

(in thousands Canadian dollars)

Note: For Canada and Mexico, income was after taxes and transfers. For the United States, income was before taxes and after transfers. For Canada, constant 1993 Canadian dollars; for the United States, 1994 U.S. dollars; for Mexico, constant 1984 pesos.

Source: Canada, Statistics Canada, Survey of Consumer Finances; Mexico, INEGI, National Income and Expenditure Survey; United States, Bureau of the Census, Current Population Survey.

United States
1984 and 1994
Percentage of Households

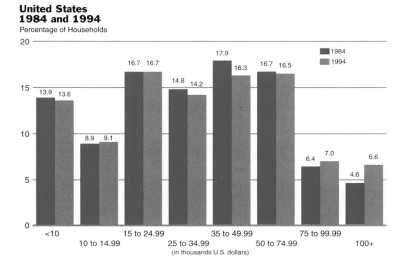

(in thousands U.S. dollars)

Mexico
1984 and 1994
Percentage of Households

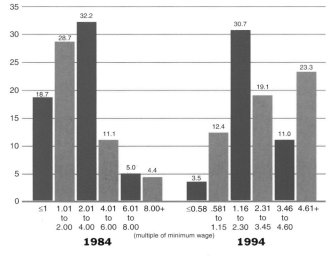

(multiple of minimum wage)

In the United States and Mexico, the major increases in income occurred for households at the top levels of income.

1984–1993. The Gini coefficient was reduced from 0.36 in 1984 to 0.35 in 1993.

In Mexico, between 1984 to 1994, there was an increase in income inequality: the Gini coefficient rose from 0.43 in 1984 to 0.48 in 1994. This situation is evident in the reduction of the share of the four lowest quintiles in the total income, while the highest quintile increased its share by 5 percentage points.

In the United States, the distribution of household income has become more unequal over the period, as shown by an increase in the Gini coefficient from 0.40 in 1984 to 0.43 in 1994. The deterioration of income distribution was mainly due to the increased income share of the top fifth of households, while the share of the other four quintiles was reduced.

Distribution of Households by Income Group in North America

One of the explanations for widening income inequality is that more households or more families and unattached individuals are moving to higher income levels at different rates. This situation exists in all three North American countries as shown in Figure 71. However, there are differences in the income groups that have benefited in each country.

In Canada, the improvement in income distribution (after taxes and transfers) was mainly due to the increased share of middle income families and individuals. Between 1984 and 1993, the share of families and individuals with incomes below Canadian $10,000 fell from 9.0 percent to 7.8 percent. The share of families and individuals with income levels ranging from $10,000 to $34,999 increased by 4.2 percentage points, while families and individuals with incomes above $35,000 decreased their share by 2.8 percentage points.

In Mexico, the share of households with income (after taxes and transfers) less than four times the minimum wage was substantially reduced during 1984–1994. This change was mainly due to a reduction in the share of households receiving less than two times the minimum wage. In contrast, the share of households receiving more than four

times the minimum wage went from 20.5 percent in 1984 to 34.3 percent in 1994, an increase of 13.8 percentage points. This result is influenced by the increasing number of earners per household during the period.

In the United States, the major increases in income (before taxes and after transfers) occurred for households at the top levels of income. During 1984–1994, the share of households receiving less than U.S.$25,000 a year remained almost unchanged; that of households between $25,000 and $75,000 was reduced by 2.4 percentage points, while the share of households with incomes above $75,000 increased by 2.6 percentage points, accounting for 13.6 percent of all households in 1994.

Real Mean Household (family and unattached individual) Income by Quintile in North America

Figure 72 shows that in Canada, real mean family and unattached individual income after taxes and transfers between 1984 and 1993 remained almost unchanged, decreasing by 1.5 percent, in contrast with the large increase during 1971–1984 (17.8 percent). The number of earners per family remained almost unchanged at 1.72 in 1993. With the exception of the lowest quintile, in which real income increased by 7.6 percent, the other four quintiles observed income stagnation. As a result, the ratio of the highest mean income quintile to the lowest mean income quintile decreased from 7.9 times in 1984 to 7.2 times in 1993, while the ratio to the other four quintiles remained unchanged over the period.

In Mexico, during 1984–1994, real mean household income after taxes and transfers increased at an average annual rate of 2.9 percent per year. Although individuals' real earnings have decreased, the household income increase was aided by the rise in earners per household from 1.58 in 1984 to 1.73 in 1994. All household quintiles increased their real mean income. However, the highest growth rate occurred in the top quintile, causing the income gap between the highest quintile and the other four quintiles to increase over this period. For example, the ratio of the mean income of the

Figure 72

Real Mean Household (family and unattached individual) Income by Quintile in North America

**Mexico
1984–1994**
Thousands in 1994 New Pesos

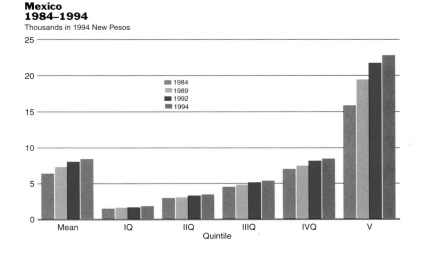

1984
1989
1992
1994

Note: Income was after taxes and after transfers in all three countries. Annual income for Canada and the United States. Quarterly income for Mexico.

Source: Canada, Statistics Canada, Survey of Employment, Payroll, and Hours; Mexico, Mexican Institute of Social Security; United States, Bureau of the Census, Current Population Survey.

**Canada
1971–1993**
Thousands in 1993 Canadian Dollars

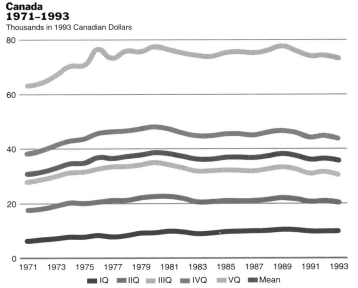

■ IQ ■ IIQ ■ IIIQ ■ IVQ ■ VQ ■ Mean

**United States
1979–1994**
Thousands in 1994 U.S. Dollars

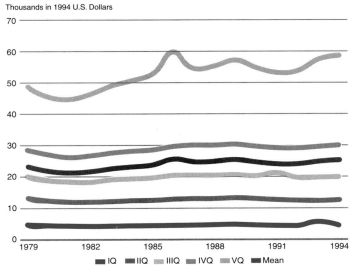

■ IQ ■ IIQ ■ IIIQ ■ IVQ ■ VQ ■ Mean

fifth quintile to the first quintile increased from 10 times in 1984 to 13 times in 1994.

In the United States, real mean household income after taxes and transfers increased by 9.5 percent during 1984–1994. Nevertheless, overall household income has not recovered from its highest level reached in 1986. Over the period, the number of earners per household remained unchanged at a level of 1.4 earners per household in 1994. Household income growth performed better than in 1979–1984 when real mean household income remained unchanged.

Because the average income of the top U.S. quintile grew at the fastest rate, consequently its ratio to the other quintiles increased. The ratio of the average income of the top 20 percent of households to the average income of the bottom 20 percent increased from 12 times in 1984 to 13 times in 1994, while its ratio to the fourth quintile increased from 1.8 to 2.0. during that same period of time.

Trends in Employment Benefits

Overview

Each country in North America has a unique combination of publicly and privately funded employment benefits that reflect its economic and social policies. The main legislated employment benefits are summarized and compared below. Available information on nonlegislated employment benefits is also presented.

In Mexico and Canada, many employment benefits and standards, such as hours of work, vacation, and maternity leave, are defined by law. In the United States, most employment benefits are established by collective bargaining between labor organizations and employers, or by company policy in nonunion firms. Another significant difference among the three countries is the extent to which health care is considered an employment benefit. Health care in Canada is not an employment benefit; it is publicly financed and universally

accessible to workers and nonworkers alike. Many larger firms provide dental benefits and supplementary health and medication plans, although those benefits are a small proportion of total employment benefits. As their name implies, such benefits are intended as a supplement to the public system.

The IMSS, which is funded by employees, employers, and government contributions in Mexico, supports health care services for wage and salary workers. Other groups of workers, such as family workers, the self-employed, employers, and small collective landholders, are also eligible for these benefits. However, they are required to pay all contributions, and very few of them have taken advantage of this eligibility. Health care for employees in the public sector is provided by the ISSSTE.

In the United States, workers' health care is considered an employment benefit and is funded largely by employers and employees. Workers whose employers do not provide this benefit can purchase private insurance, obtain insurance under a spouse's plan, or remain uninsured. These distinctions are important to keep in mind when examining trends in employment benefits.

There are some important similarities in trends in employment benefits in all three countries. Benefits are gaining greater importance as a form of compensation as they grow relative to wages and salaries. The distribution of benefits among workers is being altered as growing numbers of workers in nonstandard jobs are provided with reduced benefits or none. Benefits are taking new forms as profit-sharing and other benefit mechanisms grow in popularity and the needs of aging populations are addressed. The challenge for North American countries is to improve the living standards of workers by encouraging the development of employment benefits that are transferable from one job to another, that can benefit workers in nonstandard jobs, and that can provide adequate, lifelong benefits in a cost-effective manner. In all three countries, many programs that legislate employment benefit are under review.

Comparison of Benefits

The main sources of information for Tables 3A–3E, which compare legislated employment benefits in North America, are Human Resources Development Canada, the Mexican STPS, and the United States Department of Labor.

In Mexico, all legislated employment benefits fall under federal statutes, with enforcement shared by federal and state authorities. In Canada and the United States, these benefits are regulated by a combination of federal and either provincial or state statutes. In Canada, labor laws fall mainly within provincial authority (as property and civil rights legislation). However, federal jurisdiction over labor matters extends to areas that are national, international, or interprovincial in nature, such as railways, banks, radio and television broadcasting, and telephone and cable systems. Approximately 10 percent of the Canadian work force is covered by federal jurisdiction; the rest of the workers come under provincial law. In the United States, the federal jurisdiction prevails in the establishment of minimum standards in most areas of employment legislation, but states can set higher standards and often share in enforcement.

In all three countries, collective agreements may contain special provisions that enhance minimum legislated employment benefits.

Legislated Employment Benefits

The extent to which various benefits are legislated differs from country to country. Tables 3A–3E compare various types of benefits available to North American workers and notes the presence or absence of legislation regulating them.

Other Employment Benefits

Cost of Benefits

In all three North American countries, employment benefits are gaining in importance as a form of compensation.[7] Benefits accounted for 30.0 percent of manufacturing remuneration in Mexico in 1995. In 1992, benefits accounted for 40.3 percent of manufacturing payroll in the United States. In 1995, benefits represented 27.3 percent of total payroll in Canada and 28.4 percent of total compensation in the United States (note that the Canadian figure does not include health insurance, while the U.S. figure includes health insurance, which accounted for 6.2 percent of total compensation costs). While these data are not strictly comparable across countries, they provide an indication of benefit levels in each country.

The cost of benefits has grown significantly in all three countries over the past decade. In the United States, "other labor income," which includes employer contributions to social programs and additional private benefits, increased from 9.0 percent to 11.0 percent of total labor income between 1984 and 1994. In Canada, "supplementary labor income," which includes employer contributions to social programs and private benefits, increased from 10.0 percent to 13.0 percent during 1984–1994. In Mexico, benefit costs in manufacturing industries grew 17.8 percent in real terms during 1984–1995, and employer and employee payroll taxes for social security increased.

Distribution of Benefits

The distribution of employment benefits among the working population in North America has been significantly altered as a result of the increase in nonstandard work, the numbers of workers in small firms, and the increasing cost of benefits.[8] Employment benefits in the United States, Mexico, and Canada have largely been designed for "standard" full-time wage and salary workers. Most private employer-provided benefits, such as vacations and company pension plans, improve with a worker's seniority. However, with a higher degree of flux in the labor market, fewer workers remain with the same employer for a significant length of time. Further, with the growth in nonstandard work and in employment in small firms with fewer than 100 employees, fewer workers are gaining access to benefits.

In all three North American countries, employment benefits are gaining in importance as a form of compensation.

Table 3A

Comparison of Legislated Employment Benefits in North America: Vacations, Holidays, and Work Hours

Type of Benefits	Paid Vacations	Paid Holidays	Hours of Work
Canada	2 weeks of annual vacation after each completed year of employment at 4 percent of annual earnings; the federal and several provincial jurisdictions also provide for 3 weeks of vacation after 4–6 years of continuous employment with one employer at 6 percent of annual earnings.	Varies from 5 to 11 paid holidays annually with most provincial legislation requiring 8 or 9 days.	Standard is 8 hours/day, 40–48 hours/week with 44 hours/week being the most common. Maximum of 48 hours/week in most jurisdictions, after which overtime rates must be paid.
United States	No federally or state mandated vacation requirements. General practice: 1 week after 1 year 2 weeks after 2 years, 3 weeks after 5–10 years, and 4 weeks after 10–20 years.	No federally mandated days off for holidays in private sector, though some states have such requirements.	Legislated standard is 40 hours/week after which overtime at a rate of 150 percent must be paid; no maximum.
Mexico	6 days of vacation after one year of employment. Two additional days/year for each year thereafter up to 12 days. After 5 years the employee is entitled to 14 vacation days, and two additional days for each subsequent 5-year interval. Seasonal or occasional workers are entitled to vacation time on a prorated basis, according to the number of days worked. Workers are entitled to a bonus of not less than 25 percent of pay for the vacation period.	7 mandatory statutory holidays.	A maximum of 8 hours per day, 7 hours/night and 6.5 hours for split-shift work. Overtime limited to 3 hours/day for no more than 3 days/week at overtime premium rates (usually 150 percent).

Table 3B

Comparison of Legislated Employment Benefits in North America: Rest and Leaves

Type of Benefits	Day(s) of Rest	Maternity/Parental Leave	Other Family-Related Leaves
Canada	One full day of rest/week, preferably Sunday	17 weeks leave of absence without pay after anywhere from 1 to 26 weeks of employment service, depending on the province of residence as well as anywhere from 0 to 34 weeks of parental leave, depending on the province. Workers are entitled to be reinstated in the same or comparable position. The unemployment insurance program provides 15 weeks of maternity benefits, 10 weeks of parental benefits, and 15 weeks of sickness benefits for a maximum of 30 weeks at 55 percent of insurable earnings.	The federal and several provincial jurisdictions allow for bereavement leave for death in the immediate family, as well as unpaid sick leave and child-care leave.
United States	No general federal mandate. Some federal regulations for specific occupations; some state regulations.	No federal paid leave requirement, but federal law protects the right to return to a job after childbirth in firms with more than 50 employees. Maternity must be treated like any disability. If disability pay is provided for nonwork related injuries, it must be given for maternity leave. There is no unemployment insurance for maternity leave.	Family leave law allows workers in businesses with 50 or more employees to take up to 12 weeks of unpaid leave per year for family or medical emergencies.
Mexico	One complete day of rest with full pay, preferably Sunday.	All employees are entitled to 3 months of fully paid maternity leave. They are entitled to free medical and hospital care and to medication supported by social security payments (see Social Security below).	

In Canada, legislated benefits such as a standard 40–48 hour work week and a certain number of vacation days apply only to full-time workers with one employer. These benefits do not apply to the 15.5 percent of the labor force who are self-employed, nor to many multiple part-time job holders. Close to half of full-time employees are covered by employer-sponsored pension plans, whereas only 10.0 percent of part-time workers are covered by such plans. Less than half of all workers were eligible for unemployment insurance in 1995 as a result of the growth in part-time workers (those working less than 15 hours per week were ineligible until recently) and the self-employed. Small firms, which between 1978 and 1992 created the majority of net jobs in Canada, tend to limit employment benefits. Flexible working hours, extended maternity leave, and special family leaves are offered by 60.0 percent of the largest firms (more than 2,000 employees, but just over

Table 3C

Comparison of Legislated Employment Benefits in North America: Public Pensions

Type of Benefits	Social Security/ Public Pension Plans
Canada	Canada/Quebec Pension Plans, disability income, and death benefits are financed by a 5.6 percent payroll tax paid in equal shares by employers and employees with maximum pensionable earnings of C$35,400. Pension benefits in 1996 were 25 percent of average monthly pensionable earnings during the contribution period. Individual Registered Retirement Savings Plans can be set up privately by workers to provide tax-deferred retirement savings.
United States	A 15.3 percent payroll tax is equally shared by employers and employees. The tax supports a public pension plan, disability insurance, death benefits, and health care for those over age 65 (Medicare) with maximum insurable earnings of U.S.$62,700 in 1996. Employers and employees can opt to establish private defined benefit or contribution pension plans, which may be tax deferred.
Mexico	Wage and salary workers at IMSS receive health and maternity care, compensation for the disabled, and old age dismissal and pensions supported by a 14.7 percent employer payroll, a 3.25 percent employee payroll (employer pays full cost for employees earning the minimum wage), and a government contribution. This fund covers about 11 million wage and salary workers in the private formal sector. Child care for working women is supported by a 1 percent payroll tax on employers. About 2.2 million federal government workers have a separate but similar social security plan. An employer payroll tax of 5 percent supports the National Housing Fund, which provides low-cost housing to private wage and salaried employees. A mandatory retirement savings plan for wage and salary workers was established in 1992 funded by a 2 percent employer payroll tax.

Table 3D

Comparison of Legislated Employment Benefits in North America: Unemployment Insurance and Profit-Sharing

Type of Benefits	Unemployment Insurance	Profit-Sharing
Canada	Benefits are 55 percent of insurable earnings to a maximum of C$413/week, for up to 45 weeks. Minimum weeks of work to qualify varies between 12 and 20 weeks depending on regional unemployment rate. For new labor force entrants and reentrants 26 weeks are required. Payments are financed by employer payroll tax of 4.3 percent of insured earnings and an employee contribution of 3 percent of insured earnings. As of January 1997, minimum hours of work required will be 420–700 hours with 910 hours of work required for new entrants or reentrants. A family income supplement for low-income families will also be available. Less than half of the unemployed received benefits in 1994.	No requirement by employers to share profits with employees.
United States	State-based system provides for about 13 weeks, at 37 percent of pay on average (minimum 27 percent, maximum 52 percent) to a maximum of U.S.$180–354/week, depending on the state. Duration can be extended to 26–39 weeks in states with high unemployment or for trade adjustment. Payments are financed by an employer payroll tax that ranges from 0.6 percent to 4.9 percent (average across states is 2.2 percent) with experience rating and a federal supplement from the General Treasury. About 35 percent of unemployed received benefits in 1995.	No requirement by employers to share profits with employees.
Mexico	There is no unemployment insurance program. Severance pay is provided to formal sector workers in the case of layoffs or closures and is based on length of service and circumstances surrounding the dismissal. Generally, a lump sum equal to 3 months' pay plus 20 days' pay for each year of service is provided to workers in the formal sector. Unemployed formal sector workers are eligible for health care benefits for up to 6 months after dismissal.	Enterprises are required by law to distribute 10 percent of annual taxable income to employees. Profits are allocated in two stages: first distribution is based on days worked/year; second distribution is proportional to the workers' annual salary.

one-third of smaller firms (fewer than 500 employees) offer such benefits.

Among small firms (fewer than 100 employees) in the United States, which accounted for 39 percent of employment in 1991, 30 percent of full-time workers did not participate in employer-provided health care plans, 12 percent did not receive paid vacations, 18 percent did not receive paid holidays, and 47 percent did not receive paid sick leave. In 1992, 55 percent of full-time workers and 88 percent of part-time workers did not have retirement plans. Also in 1992, 72 percent of small employers did not provide unpaid maternity leave. In large and medium-sized firms, 8 percent of full-time workers did not receive paid vacations and

holidays, 33 percent did not receive paid sick leave, 63 percent did not receive unpaid maternity leave, and 22 percent did not receive a retirement plan in 1992. About 50 percent of private wage and salary workers in the United States who work 1–20 hours per week lacked employer-sponsored health care coverage, compared with 26 percent working 21–34 hours per week and 3 percent of those working more than 35 hours per week. About 49 percent of employees working for temporary help agencies had health insurance available to them, although less than 10 percent actually participated in the plan. Similarly, 74 percent of these U.S. workers had holiday and vacation plans available to them, but fewer than 10 percent qualified for these

Table 3E

Comparison of Legislated Employment Benefits in North America: Worker's Compensation

Type of Benefits	Worker's Compensation
Canada	Provincially based systems provide no-fault worker's compensation benefits. Federal system, tied to provincial system, provides benefits for workers in the federal jurisdiction. Insurable earnings ranged from C$35,000 to C$55,600, and maximum benefit levels ranged from 75 percent to 90 percent of net insurable earnings in 1995. The system is supported by an employer payroll tax of between 1.4 percent and 3 percent, depending on the province.
United States	State-based system generally provides for two-thirds of salary for duration of disability and provides schedule of specified benefits for certain injuries. Maximum weekly benefit ranges from U.S.$275–846, depending on the state. Worker's compensation is optional in some states. The system is financed by employer payroll taxes with experience rating and uses no federal standards or funding.
Mexico	Compensation for job-related accidents and illnesses is supported through mandated employer contributions, which are part of the social security system.

Source: Canada, "Employment Standards Legislation," Human Resources Development Canada, 1995–1996; Mexico, IMSS and STPS; United States, Department of Labor, Bureau of National Affairs, and the AFL–CIO.

benefits in 1994. Agencies typically require 1,000 hours of service in a year to qualify for benefits. In 1993, 58 percent of the population had employer-sponsored health insurance, compared with 66 percent in 1980, despite increases in employer expenditures on health care over this period.

In Mexico, 34 percent of the labor force received benefits in 1995, compared with 39 percent in 1991. This change was mainly because of the growth in the numbers of nonstandard and unpaid workers. About 63 percent of salary workers received social security benefits in 1993, down from 66 percent in 1991. Only 29 percent of piece workers had benefits in 1993. These workers have increased their share from 9 percent of all salary workers in 1991 to 11 percent of all salary workers in 1995. Among nonsalary workers such as the self-employed, employers, and unpaid workers, who in 1995 accounted for almost 45 percent of total employment, only 2 percent received employment benefits. Under the Social Insurance Law of the Mexican Institute for Social Security, these workers are permitted to join the obligatory insurance regime and receive social security services if they pay the total required contribution themselves. These workers rely on publicly financed systems for health care and other benefits.

Types of Workers
Greater benefits go to higher paid, more-educated workers in professional occupations and in sectors such as manufacturing and public administration.[9]

In Canada, supplementary labor income (including employer-paid benefits, such as pensions, unemployment insurance, worker's compensation, disability insurance, etc.) of manufacturing workers represented 15.3 percent of total labor income in 1994, compared with 9.0 percent for service workers. Professional and technical employees had the greatest access to family-supportive work arrangements, such as child care, family leave, and flexible hours, while unskilled workers had the least access. Canadians least likely to be satisfied with their maternity and pension benefits are those who work in small firms, are under 35 years of age, and earn

lower incomes. Those who are most satisfied tend to be in larger firms (more than 500 employees); in technical, professional, or managerial occupations; in a unionized firm; and in jobs earning higher incomes.

In Mexico, the percentage of professional, technical, and managerial workers with benefits dropped from 82 percent in 1991 to 76 percent in 1993, compared with a drop from 42 percent to 39 percent during that period for service and domestic workers with benefits. In 1995, the majority of workers in agriculture, hotels, restaurants, transportation, business, and other services had no benefits, while a majority of workers in manufacturing, utilities, and public administration had benefits. Access to benefits increased with earnings in Mexico for workers earning less than 10 times the minimum wage. For example, in 1995, 91 percent of workers earning less than the minimum wage had no benefits compared with 58 percent of workers earning one to two times the minimum wage.

In the United States, health care coverage for workers with a college degree dropped from 79 percent to 73 percent between 1979 and 1993, while coverage for workers with less than a high school education dropped from 52 percent to 36 percent coverage during the same period. Similarly in 1993, 27 percent of workers with family incomes below U.S.$10,000 were ineligible for or were denied employer-sponsored health care coverage, compared with 6 percent of workers with family incomes above U.S.$40,000.

Profit-Sharing and Pension Plans
One growing type of benefit is profit-sharing in the form of cash or deferred plans. Another important development is the growing popularity of defined contribution pension plans in Canada and the United States.[10]

In 1990, about 12 percent of Canadian employees participated in cash profit-sharing schemes, which were available in 15 percent of firms with more than 20 employees. Also in 1990, fewer than 8 percent of employees participated in the formal deferred profit-sharing plans offered by 4 percent

In Mexico, cash-based profit-sharing is obligatory by law for most enterprises at 10 percent of annual taxable income.

of firms with more than 20 employees. Cash-based schemes increased by at least one-third in the 1980s, while deferred plans declined.

In Mexico, cash-based profit-sharing is obligatory by law for all enterprises, excluding new enterprises, the mining industry, private assistance institutions, public assistance institutions, and enterprises with less than a certain amount of capital. All workers, with the exception of directors, management, and domestic employees, are covered. Profit-sharing is fixed at 10 percent of annual taxable income.

In the United States in 1993, 3.0 percent of firms with more than 100 employees have cash-based profit-sharing plans, and 15.0 percent of firms with more than 100 employees have deferred profit-sharing plans. In contrast with Canada, there was no significant increase in cash-based plans in the United States during 1985–1989. However, deferred plans increased fourfold from 1969 to 1989. Only 0.4 percent of payroll was spent on profit-sharing in 1993, and 0.3 percent on stock bonus and employee stock ownership plans.

While defined benefit pension plans continue to be the dominant form of employer-provided pension plans in both Canada and the United States, defined contribution pension plans are growing in importance. In the United States during 1980–1987, the proportion of private-sector workers with defined benefit pension plans declined from 38 percent to 31 percent, while the proportion of these workers with defined contribution pension plans grew from 8 percent to 15 percent. In Canada, the shift has been less dramatic. In 1986–1994, the proportion of private-sector workers with defined benefit, registered pension plans dropped from 27 percent to 25 percent, while the proportion with defined contribution or hybrid registered plans grew from 4 percent to 5 percent.

In Mexico, the national pension system (SAR) was modified in 1996. By July 1997, the pension contributions that will be paid by employers, workers, and the government to Mexico's grant security agency will be redirected to individual accounts managed by private companies called AFORES (Administradoras de Fondos Para el Retiro de los Trabajadore). Under this new pension system, workers will have the option to choose among different investment plans that are presented by the AFORES.

Endnotes

[1] OECD. *Employment Outlook*. See especially Chapter 3, "Earnings Inequality, Low-Pay Employment, and Earnings Mobility," in July 1996.

[2] The low proportion of wage and salary workers in total employment in Mexico might explain the low share of labor income in the GDP, compared to Canada and the United States. In 1995, wage and salary workers accounted for 59 percent of total employment, while the share for the United States and Canada was 92 and 84 percent, respectively.

[3] It refers to full-time wage and salary workers of 25 years and over.

[4] Ernest B. Akyeampong, "Working for the Minimum Wage," in *Perspectives*, Statistics Canada, Winter 1989.

[5] In October 1996, the U.S. federal minimum wage was increased to $4.75 per hour. From January 1, 1996, to March 31, 1996, the average Mexican minimum wage was 18.43 pesos per day. In April 1996, it was increased to 20.66 pesos per day. It should be noted that in Mexico the Labor Law establishes that for each six days of work, workers will have a day of rest with full pay.

[6] The legal minimum wage is established on a yearly basis by a tripartite commission consisting of workers, employer, and government representatives.

[7] Some of the data supporting this discussion of benefits as a form of compensation come from National Income and Expenditure Accounts, *Conference Board of Canada Compensation Planning Outlook*, 1996; Mexico's National Income and Expenditure Survey and Monthly Industrial Survey; U.S. National Income and Product Accounts; Bureau of National Affairs [an independent U.S. publisher of business and labor reports], *Benefit Costs and Practices*, 1995; and the U.S. Department of Labor, "Report on the American Workforce," 1994 and 1995.

[8] Some of the data supporting this discussion of the distribution of employment benefits come from Statistic

Canada's National Income and Expenditure Accounts, *Conference Board of Canada Compensation Planning Outlook*, 1996; Human Resources Development Canada, *Statistics Canada Working Paper Series, No. 71*; Mexico's National Commission for Minimum Wages and INEGI, 1993, and the ENE; U.S. Department of Labor, Bureau of Labor Statistics, "Survey of Employee Benefits in Small Establishments," 1992; U.S. Department of Labor, Bureau of Labor Statistics, "Report on the American Workforce," 1994 and 1995; H. Stein and M. Foss, *The American Economy*, 1995, AEI Press; and Bureau of National Affairs, *Benefit Costs and Practices, 1995*.

[9] Some of the data supporting this discussion of the relationship between education level and benefits come from Statistics Canada, National Income and Product Accounts; National Childcare Survey; "Decima Workplace Survey in Canada," 1992; Mexico's ENE; and the U.S. Department of Labor, Bureau of Labor Statistics, "Report on the American Workforce," 1995.

[10] Some of the data supporting this discussion of profit-sharing and defined contribution pension plans come from the OECD Employment Outlook, 1995; U.S. Department of Labor, Bureau of Labor Statistics, 1992; and the U.S. Chamber of Commerce Study of Employer's 1993 Benefit Costs.

Suggested Improvements to Data Comparability

Preparation of this profile of labor markets in North America uncovered several issues related to comparability of information among the three countries, as noted in each of the chapter overviews. Some of these issues are elaborated on in the bulleted section below.

Employment Data

- **Employment Definition:** There is need for greater compatibility of definitions of "employed" workers among the three countries (see Chapter II, Data Issues: Employment, pages 28–29).

- **Self-Employment:** Data separating self-employed workers in the United States (both incorporated and unincorporated) into two categories—those with employees and those without employees—would be helpful for comparison purposes.

- **Nonstandard Workers:** As noted in Chapter II, part-time, temporary, and self-employed workers are defined differently by the three countries. For comparison purposes, it would be helpful to collect comparable data in this area given the tremendous growth in nonstandard workers in all three countries over the past several years and the important implications this change has for labor market policy.

- **Training:** There has been significant interest in gathering more information on training, given its increased importance in determining labor market outcomes. Mexico has a special survey on education, training, and employment that is conducted every two years at the same time as the National Employment Survey. This survey has extensive detailed information on training by worker occupation, industry, age, gender, level of instruction, and source of training. One of the major problems is to identify which training was received for working purposes. U.S. training data from the Department of Labor are based on a survey of establishments rather than workers. As a result, there is a lack of national data on the training experience of workers. In Canada, the Adult Education and Training Survey (a survey of workers), provides information on worker training. The data are not as extensive as that available in Mexico in terms of detailed industry and occupational breakdowns, duration, number and type of courses received, and reasons for taking training.

- **Unionization:** Information on unionization in Mexico at the national level by age, gender, industry, and occupation through a household employment survey would support comparative analyses. In all three countries, more precise information on categories of workers who are "unionizable" or "not unionizable" would also help comparative analysis.

Unemployment Data

- **Unemployment Definition:** The definition of "unemployed" workers varies significantly among the three countries (see Chapter III, Data Issues: Unemployment and Underemployment, pages 68–69). A greater degree of harmony in definition would improve comparability.

- **Duration:** More consistent unemployment duration intervals among the three countries would improve comparability.

- **Job Flux:** For all three countries, more information on the movement of workers from job to job, with periods of unemployment or periods when they left the labor force, would be helpful. Job gain and job loss information by year for the United States and Mexico would allow three-way comparisons. This information would provide a better sense of the degree of job flux in the three labor markets.

- **Composition:** Categorizing unemployed workers in Mexico as "reentrants" would facilitate comparisons to the United States and Canada.

Earnings, Benefits, and Income Distribution Data

- **Earnings:** Numerous differences exist in the coverage of earnings data among the three countries as described in Chapter IV. Earnings data covering all workers (including full-time, part-time, self-employed, and supervisory workers) in all industries by gender and age would facilitate comparisons among the three countries and with other OECD countries.

- **Minimum-Wage Workers:** Current information on the number and characteristics of Canadian workers who earn the minimum wage or less as a measure of possible economic hardship or underemployment would be helpful.

- **Income Distribution:** There are several difficulties in comparing income distribution data among the three countries as noted in Chapter IV. The following information would improve future analyses: household income distribution data for Canada, on an after tax and transfer basis; income distribution data before taxes and after transfers for Mexico.

- **Benefits:** In all three countries, monetary and nonmonetary benefits are a growing share of income for workers, yet detailed comparable data on benefits are generally not available. It would be particularly helpful to gather better information at a national level on the types and levels of benefits that workers receive across variables such as industry, occupation, hours of work, and unionization. It would also be useful to gather information on the benefits of different types of workers such as the self-employed, workers paid hourly wages, salary workers, part-time workers, full-time workers, temporary workers, etc.

- **Labor Productivity:** In the manufacturing sector, it would be useful to have Mexican data covering all manufacturing industries at the national level.

APPENDIX B

Statistical Tables 1–5

Table 1

Macroeconomic Statistics for North American Countries
1984–1995*

	1984	1985	1986	1987	1988	1989	1990	1991	1992	1993	1994	1995
Real Gross Domestic Product[a]												
Annual Change												
Canada	6.3	4.8	3.3	4.2	5.0	2.4	−0.2	−1.8	0.8	2.2	4.1	2.3
Mexico	3.6	2.6	−3.8	1.9	1.3	3.3	4.5	3.6	2.8	0.7	3.5	−6.9
United States	6.7	3.2	2.9	3.1	3.9	2.5	1.2	−0.6	2.3	3.1	4.1	2.1
Real Gross Domestic Investment[a]												
Annual Change												
Canada	2.1	9.5	6.2	10.8	10.3	6.1	−3.6	−2.9	−1.5	0.6	7.2	−1.4
Mexico	6.4	7.9	−11.8	−0.1	5.8	6.4	13.1	8.3	10.8	−1.2	8.1	−29.8
United States	...	6.2	1.5	0.3	2.7	0.6	−0.1	−6.1	5.4	9.3	9.9	...
Total % of GDP												
Canada	18.7	19.5	20.1	21.4	22.4	23.2	22.5	22.2	21.7	21.4	22.0	18.3
Mexico	17.1	17.9	16.4	16.1	16.8	17.3	18.7	19.5	21.1	20.7	21.7	16.1
United States	19.3	19.9	19.6	19.0	18.8	18.5	18.2	17.2	17.7	18.8	19.8	...
Exports of Goods and Services[b]												
(in billions of U.S. dollars)												
Canada	105.2	106.7	106.5	119.3	140.9	150.9	157.8	156.4	161.8	173.2	197.2	227.4
Mexico	37.8	35.9	29.9	37.4	42.1	48.1	56.1	58.1	61.7	67.8	78.6	97.5
United States	290.9	288.8	309.5	348.0	430.2	489.0	537.6	581.2	617.7	643.0	698.3	786.5
Total % of GDP[c]												
Canada	26.7	27.0	27.3	27.1	28.3	27.9	29.1	30.0	32.1	34.6	37.8	41.8
Mexico	16.4	15.3	16.7	17.9	18.7	18.5	18.3	18.5	18.3	18.9	19.6	26.9
United States	7.4	7.2	7.5	8.0	8.9	9.8	10.4	11.1	11.6	11.7	12.3	11.5
Imports of Goods and Services[d]												
(in billions of U.S. dollars)												
Canada	105.8	111.2	116.6	131.1	158.0	173.6	179.4	180.0	183.2	195.4	213.4	235.6
Mexico	33.6	35.1	31.3	33.1	44.5	53.9	63.5	72.7	86.1	91.2	108.0	98.2
United States	400.1	410.9	448.3	500.0	545.0	579.3	616.0	609.1	655.9	715.0	802.7	891.6

*See footnotes at the end of table.

	1984	1985	1986	1987	1988	1989	1990	1991	1992	1993	1994	1995
Total % of GDP[e]												
Canada	24.4	25.3	26.5	27.1	29.4	30.5	31.1	32.8	34.3	36.5	39.1	41.6
Mexico	6.9	7.5	7.2	7.4	10.0	11.8	13.5	15.1	17.8	17.5	19.1	14.8
United States	10.3	10.6	11.0	11.2	11.1	11.3	11.5	11.5	12.3	13.2	14.4	13.1
Trade Balance												
(in billions of U.S. dollars)												
Canada	15.3	12.0	7.1	8.5	7.2	5.1	7.5	3.2	5.1	7.2	10.9	20.7
Mexico	13.2	8.4	5.0	8.8	2.6	0.4	−0.9	−7.3	−15.9	−13.5	−18.5	7.1
United States	−112.5	−122.2	−145.1	−159.6	−127.0	−115.3	−109.0	−73.8	−96.1	−132.6	−166.1	−174.0
Index of Consumer Prices[f] **Annual Growth**												
Canada	4.4	3.9	4.2	4.4	4.0	5.0	4.8	5.6	1.5	1.8	0.2	2.1
Mexico	65.5	57.7	86.2	131.8	114.2	20.0	26.7	22.7	15.5	9.8	7.0	35.0
United States	3.2	4.3	3.6	1.9	3.6	4.1	4.8	5.4	4.2	3.0	3.0	2.9

Notes:

... = not available

For more information about the data, see comparability and definitional issues in Chapter I.

[a] Data on national currency basis.

[b] On balance of payments basis.

[c] Total exports of goods and services as percentage of GDP. On national currency basis at constant prices.

[d] On balance of payments basis.

[e] Total imports of goods and services as percentage of GDP. On national currency basis at constant prices.

[f] Index of consumer prices annual growth from January to December of each year.

Sources: Canada, Statistics Canada, National Income and Expenditure Accounts; Mexico, INEGI, System of National Accounts United States, Bureau of the Census, National Income and Product Accounts.

Table 2

Population and Labor Force Statistics for North American Countries 1984–1995

	1984	1985	1986	1987	1988	1989	1990	1991	1992	1993	1994	1995
Population (in thousands)												
Canada	25,702	25,942	26,204	26,550	26,895	27,379	27,791	28,120	28,542	28,941	29,248	29,558
Mexico	76,222	76,771	77,324	77,881	78,442	79,833	81,250	83,265	85,250	86,613	88,371	90,164
United States	236,393	238,510	240,691	242,860	245,093	247,397	249,951	252,699	255,472	257,713	260,257	262,688
Working Age Population (in thousands)												
Canada	19,683	19,843	20,177	20,436	20,685	20,964	21,291	21,601	21,976	22,386	22,714	23,103
Mexico	43,629	44,620	45,633	46,669	47,728	49,146	50,607	52,111	53,296	54,507	56,016	57,573
United States	176,311	178,181	180,450	182,721	184,627	186,269	187,932	189,853	191,526	193,414	196,781	198,351
Labor Force (in thousands)												
Canada												
Total	12,853	13,123	13,377	13,630	13,901	14,151	14,329	14,408	14,482	14,663	14,832	14,961
Male	7,453	7,551	7,656	7,737	7,826	7,934	7,970	7,970	7,997	8,078	8,174	8,220
Female	5,400	5,572	5,721	5,893	6,075	6,217	6,359	6,438	6,485	6,585	6,658	6,741
Mexico												
Total	22,998	24,019	25,040	26,061	27,082	28,103	29,125	30,146	31,264	32,383	33,354	34,325
Male	16,683	17,282	17,881	18,480	19,079	19,678	20,280	20,876	21,569	22,262	22,762	23,263
Female	6,315	6,737	7,159	7,581	8,003	8,425	8,845	9,270	9,695	10,121	10,592	11,062
United States												
Total	113,544	115,461	117,835	119,865	121,669	123,870	124,788	125,303	126,982	128,040	131,056	132,300
Male	63,835	64,411	65,422	66,207	66,927	67,840	68,234	68,411	69,184	69,633	70,817	71,427
Female	49,709	51,050	52,413	53,658	54,742	56,030	56,554	56,893	57,798	58,407	60,239	60,871
Labor Force Participation Rate (%)												
Canada												
Total	65.3	65.8	66.3	66.7	67.2	67.5	67.3	66.7	65.9	65.5	65.3	64.8
Male	76.9	77.0	77.1	77.0	77.0	77.1	76.3	75.1	74.0	73.5	73.3	72.8
Female	54.0	55.1	55.8	56.7	57.7	58.3	58.7	58.5	58.0	57.9	57.6	57.6
Mexico												
Total	52.7	53.8	54.9	55.8	56.7	57.2	57.6	57.8	58.7	59.4	59.5	59.6
Male	79.6	81.0	82.3	83.5	84.7	84.6	84.4	84.1	84.6	85.0	84.5	84.0
Female	27.8	28.9	29.9	30.9	31.7	32.6	33.3	34.0	34.9	35.8	36.4	37.0

	1984	1985	1986	1987	1988	1989	1990	1991	1992	1993	1994	1995

Labor Force Participation Rate (%)

United States

Total	64.4	64.8	65.3	65.6	65.9	66.5	66.4	66.0	66.3	66.2	66.6	66.7
Male	76.4	76.3	76.3	76.2	76.2	76.4	76.1	75.5	75.6	75.2	75.1	75.2
Female	53.6	54.5	55.3	56.0	56.6	57.4	57.5	57.3	57.8	57.9	58.8	58.9

Notes: For more information about the data, see comparability and definitional issues in each chapter.

For Mexico, data from 1985 to 1990, 1992, and 1994 were estimated on the basis of trends observed in survey years. Canadian total population for 1995 was estimated. For the United States, data for 1994 and 1995 are not directly comparable with previous years data.

Sources: Canada, Statistics Canada, Census and Labor Force Survey; Mexico, INEGI, General Census of Households and Population and National Income and Expenditure Survey, STPS/INEGI, National Employment Survey; United States, Bureau of the Census, Census; Bureau of Labor Statistics, Current Population Survey.

Employment Statistics for North American Countries 1984–1995*

	1984	1985	1986	1987	1988	1989	1990	1991	1992	1993	1994	1995
Employment[a] (in thousands)												
Total												
Canada	11,402	11,742	12,095	12,422	12,819	13,086	13,165	12,916	12,842	13,015	13,292	13,506
Mexico	21,986	23,187	24,189	25,253	26,413	27,456	28,481	29,479	30,577	31,583	32,352	32,673
United States	105,005	107,150	109,597	112,440	114,968	117,342	117,914	116,877	117,598	119,306	123,060	124,676
Male												
Canada	6,615	6,764	6,933	7,075	7,247	7,356	7,320	7,104	7,031	7,126	7,290	7,397
Mexico	16,109	16,691	17,293	17,918	18,565	19,191	19,839	20,511	21,167	21,782	22,205	22,183
United States	59,091	59,891	60,892	62,107	63,273	64,315	64,435	63,593	63,805	64,700	66,450	67,379
Female												
Canada	4,787	4,978	5,162	5,347	5,572	5,730	5,845	5,812	5,811	5,889	6,002	6,109
Mexico	6,082	6,490	6,906	7,322	7,739	8,145	8,547	8,968	9,381	9,801	10,167	10,491
United States	45,915	47,259	48,706	50,334	51,696	53,027	53,479	53,284	53,793	54,606	56,610	57,297
Employment by Sector[b] (in thousands)												
Canada												
Primary	603	584	582	585	569	552	551	572	543	558	546	554
Secondary	2,824	2,867	2,938	3,020	3,169	3,233	3,117	2,868	2,758	2,739	2,856	2,956
Tertiary	7,976	8,291	8,575	8,817	9,081	9,301	9,497	9,476	9,542	9,718	9,890	9,995
Mexico[c]												
Primary	7,057	...	...	...	...	...	...	7,606	...	8,130	...	7,687
Secondary	4,551	...	...	...	...	...	...	6,897	...	7,103	...	7,101
Tertiary	10,377	...	...	...	...	...	...	14,975	...	16,351	...	17,886
United States												
Primary	3,469	3,338	3,350	3,400	3,326	3,378	3,355	3,390	3,379	3,257	3,586	3,647
Secondary	28,617	28,805	29,130	29,209	29,676	30,051	29,610	28,254	27,649	27,446	28,319	28,670
Tertiary	72,919	75,006	77,117	79,831	81,966	83,912	84,948	85,231	86,570	88,602	91,153	92,359
Employment by Class of Worker (in thousands)												
Canada												
Employees	9,773	10,065	10,413	10,676	10,998	11,277	11,276	10,996	10,906	10,958	11,181	11,370
Self-employed	1,514	1,573	1,584	1,653	1,743	1,741	1,822	1,855	1,873	1,984	2,055	2,079
Unpaid Family Workers	115	103	98	93	78	68	67	64	63	73	56	57

See footnotes at the end of table.

	1984	1985	1986	1987	1988	1989	1990	1991	1992	1993	1994	1995

Employment by Class of Worker (in thousands)

Mexico[c]

	1984	1985	1986	1987	1988	1989	1990	1991	1992	1993	1994	1995
Employers	945	...	...	...	...	...	...	2,392	...	1,348	...	1,463
Employees	13,433	...	...	...	...	...	...	16,524	...	17,762	...	19,078
Self-employed	5,452	...	...	...	...	...	...	7,178	...	8,720	...	8,522
Unpaid Family Workers	2,089	...	...	...	...	...	...	3,309	...	3,718	...	3,582
United States												
Employees	95,119	97,407	99,847	102,403	104,642	106,924	107,394	106,192	107,236	108,648	112,232	114,029
Self-employed	9,338	9,269	9,327	9,624	9,917	10,008	10,161	10,341	10,018	10,335	10,648	10,485
Unpaid Family Workers	548	474	423	413	409	410	359	344	345	323	180	158

Notes:

... = not available

For more information about the data, see comparability and definitional issues in Chapter II.

[a] Employment data for Mexico among 1985-1990, 1992, and 1993. Because of the introduction of a major redesign of the Current Population Survey in January 1994, data for the United States for 1994 and 1995 are not directly comparable with previous years.

[b] Primary sector includes agriculture, fishing, forestry, and trapping; secondary sector includes mining, manufacture, and construction; and tertiary sector includes transportation, utililities, communications, trade, financial, and social services. For the United States, data for 1994 and 1995 are not directly comparable with previous years data.

[c] Data might not be equal to the total because of nonspecifications.

Sources: Canada, Statistics Canada, Labor Force Survey; Mexico, INEGI, National Income and Expenditure Survey and STPS/INEGI, National Employment Survey; United States, Bureau of Labor Statistics, Current Population Survey.

Table 4

Unemployment Statistics for North America
1984–1995*

	1984	1985	1986	1987	1988	1989	1990	1991	1992	1993	1994	1995
Unemployment[a] (in thousands)												
Total												
Canada	1,450	1,381	1,283	1,208	1,081	1,065	1,164	1,492	1,640	1,649	1,541	1,422
Mexico	1,012	830	846	799	677	640	641	667	688	800	996	1,652
United States	8,539	8,312	8,237	7,425	6,701	6,528	6,874	8,426	9,384	8,734	7,996	7,413
Male												
Canada	838	787	723	662	578	578	649	866	966	952	885	801
Mexico	779	583	592	539	413	360	343	365	373	480	571	1,080
United States	4,724	4,509	4,514	4,105	3,681	3,528	3,821	4,789	5,396	4,944	4,391	4,000
Female												
Canada	612	594	560	546	503	487	515	626	674	697	656	621
Mexico	233	247	253	259	264	281	298	302	315	320	425	572
United States	3,815	3,803	3,723	3,320	3,020	3,000	3,053	3,637	3,988	3,790	3,605	3,413
Unemployment Rate[a] (% of labor force)												
Total												
Canada	11.3	10.5	9.6	8.9	7.8	7.5	8.1	10.4	11.3	11.2	10.4	9.5
Mexico	4.4	3.5	3.4	3.1	2.5	2.3	2.2	2.2	2.2	2.5	3.0	4.8
United States	7.5	7.2	7.0	6.2	5.5	5.3	5.5	6.7	7.4	6.8	6.1	5.6
Male												
Canada	11.2	10.4	9.4	8.6	7.4	7.3	8.1	10.9	12.1	11.8	10.8	9.8
Mexico	4.7	3.8	3.1	2.5	2.0	1.9	1.8	1.7	1.9	2.1	3.1	4.6
United States	7.4	7.0	6.9	6.2	5.5	5.2	5.6	7.0	7.8	7.1	6.2	5.6
Female												
Canada	11.3	10.7	9.8	9.3	8.3	7.8	8.1	9.7	10.4	10.6	9.9	9.2
Mexico	3.8	3.7	3.5	3.4	3.3	3.3	3.4	3.4	3.2	3.1	4.0	5.2
United States	7.6	7.4	7.1	6.2	5.6	5.4	5.4	6.3	6.9	6.5	6.0	5.7
Duration of Unemployment[b] (average weeks per year)												
Canada	21.5	21.6	20.3	20.5	18.2	17.8	16.8	19.3	22.6	25.1	25.7	18.9
Mexico	5.1	6.9	5.5	6.3	6.4	6.0	5.9	5.8	5.7	5.9	5.7	5.8
United States	18.2	15.6	15.0	14.5	13.5	11.9	12.1	13.8	17.9	18.1	18.8	16.8

See footnotes at the end of table.

	1984	1985	1986	1987	1988	1989	1990	1991	1992	1993	1994	1995
Discouraged Workers[b] (% of labor force)												
Canada	1.2	0.9	0.8	0.7	0.5	0.5	0.0	0.6	0.7	0.8	...	...
Mexico	...	...	...	2.1	1.8	1.5	1.6	1.5	1.8	2.2	2.4	2.4
United States	1.1	1.0	1.0	0.9	0.8	0.7	0.7	0.8	0.9	0.9	0.4	0.3
Unemployment by Labor Experience[b] (% of total unemployment)												
Canada												
Experienced	95.2	95.7	96.0	96.0	96.8	97.0	97.3	97.0	96.2	95.3	95.1	...
Inexperienced	4.8	4.3	4.1	4.0	3.2	3.0	2.7	3.0	3.8	4.7	4.9	...
Mexico												
Experienced	67.7	73.2	77.2	76.0	73.8	76.0	78.7	82.3	85.4	83.7	85.3	87.4
Inexperienced	32.3	26.8	22.8	24.0	26.2	24.0	21.3	17.7	14.6	16.3	14.7	12.6
United States												
Experienced	87.0	87.5	87.4	87.6	87.8	89.6	90.3	90.8	90.3	89.7	92.4	92.1
Inexperienced	13.0	12.5	12.5	12.4	12.2	10.4	9.8	9.2	9.7	10.3	7.6	7.8

Notes:

... = not available

For more information about the data, see comparability and conceptual issues in Chapter III.

[a] Unemployment data for Mexico among 1985–1990, 1992, and 1993 were estimated. Because of the introduction of a major redesign of the Current Population Survey in January 1994, data for the United States for 1994 and 1995 are not directly comparable with previous years.

[b] Data for Mexico are for urban areas. The coverage of the National Urban Employment Survey changed in 1984 to 1995.

Sources: Canada, Statistics Canada, Labor Force Survey; Mexico, INEGI, National Income and Expenditure Survey and STPS/INEGI, National Employment Survey; United States, Bureau of Labor Statistics, Current Population Survey.

Table 5

Earnings, Hourly Compensation Costs, Labor Productivity, and Income Distribution Statistics in North American Countries 1984–1995*

	1984	1985	1986	1987	1988	1989	1990	1991	1992	1993	1994	1995
Minimum Wage[a] (in national currency)												
Canada	4.00	4.00	4.00	4.55	4.75	5.00	5.35	5.75	6.03	6.35	6.35	...
Mexico	0.66	1.23	1.76	3.85	7.22	8.14	9.34	10.95	12.08	13.06	13.97	16.29
United States	3.35	3.35	3.35	3.35	3.35	3.35	3.80	4.25	4.25	4.25	4.25	4.25
Average Weekly Earnings[b] (in national currency)												
Canada	398.10	412.02	424.25	440.26	459.75	483.31	505.14	528.60	547.01	556.76	567.11	572.40
Mexico	8.63	13.69	23.56	49.20	99.25	127.01	159.81	201.52	243.19	289.04	347.20	395.64
United States	326.00	343.00	358.00	373.00	385.00	399.00	415.00	430.00	445.00	463.00	467.00	479.00
Labor Income as % of GDP[c]												
Canada	58.23	58.51	59.04	58.85	58.75	58.96	60.56	62.26	62.82	61.95	61.09	...
Mexico	28.70	28.70	28.50	26.80	26.20	25.70	25.00	25.80	27.30	28.50	28.80	...
United States	54.11	54.45	54.64	55.25	55.21	54.68	55.14	55.05	55.44	54.73	54.07	...
Hourly Compensation Cost in Manufacturing[d] (in U.S. dollars)												
Canada	11.14	10.94	11.10	12.04	13.50	14.77	15.83	17.16	17.03	16.40	15.95	16.00
Mexico	...	2.30	1.66	1.77	2.22	2.67	3.06	3.70	4.50	5.21	5.33	3.20
United States	12.55	13.01	13.26	13.52	13.91	14.32	14.91	15.58	16.09	16.51	16.86	17.20
Labor Productivity in Manufacturing[e] **Annual Growth**												
Canada	8.50	2.90	−1.60	0.90	0.50	0.40	1.70	0.40	3.90	1.80	3.70	1.60
Mexico	...	...	...	2.70	3.80	6.90	6.30	5.70	5.60	8.40	11.30	...
United States	1.20	3.20	2.30	6.80	2.30	0.50	1.80	2.30	2.10	3.60	4.30	3.50
Shares of Total Household Income by Quintile (after tax and after transfers)												
Canada[f]												
Lowest Fifth	5.20	5.40	5.40	5.50	5.50	5.60	5.60	5.60	5.50	5.70	...	...
Second Fifth	11.40	11.40	11.30	11.40	11.50	11.60	11.50	11.50	11.50	11.40	...	...
Third Fifth	17.80	17.60	17.50	17.50	17.50	17.60	17.50	17.30	17.50	17.20	...	...
Fourth Fifth	24.80	24.80	24.80	24.60	24.70	24.50	24.70	24.60	24.70	24.70	...	...
Highest Fifth	40.80	40.80	40.90	40.90	40.70	40.70	40.60	41.10	40.80	41.10	...	...

*See footnotes at the end of table.

	1984	1985	1986	1987	1988	1989	1990	1991	1992	1993	1994	1995

Shares of Total Household Income by Quintile (after tax and after transfers)

Mexico

	1984	1985	1986	1987	1988	1989	1990	1991	1992	1993	1994	1995
Lowest Fifth	4.83	...	...	...	...	4.39	...	...	4.30	...	4.40	...
Second Fifth	9.53	...	...	...	...	8.47	...	...	8.40	...	8.30	...
Third Fifth	14.26	...	...	...	...	13.19	...	...	12.80	...	12.70	...
Fourth Fifth	21.88	...	...	...	...	20.40	...	...	20.30	...	20.10	...
Highest Fifth	49.50	...	...	...	...	53.55	...	...	54.20	...	54.50	...

United States

	1984	1985	1986	1987	1988	1989	1990	1991	1992	1993	1994	1995
Lowest Fifth	3.70	3.70	3.50	3.70	3.70	3.80	3.70	3.70	3.60	3.40	3.50	3.70
Second Fifth	10.60	10.40	10.00	10.40	10.40	10.40	10.40	10.40	10.20	9.50	9.80	10.00
Third Fifth	16.80	16.70	16.00	16.70	16.60	16.40	16.60	16.60	16.50	16.00	15.90	16.10
Fourth Fifth	24.60	24.30	24.60	24.40	24.10	24.20	24.60	24.50	24.10	24.10	24.00	23.80
Highest Fifth	44.20	44.90	47.20	44.60	44.90	45.40	45.10	44.70	45.20	46.70	46.80	46.40

Average Earners/Household

	1984	1985	1986	1987	1988	1989	1990	1991	1992	1993	1994	1995
Canada	1.72	1.73	1.75	1.82	1.82	1.83	1.79	1.75	1.72	1.72	...	...
Mexico	1.58	...	...	...	...	1.67	...	...	1.69	...	1.73	...
United States	1.41	1.41	1.42	1.42	1.42	1.43	1.42	1.40	1.39	1.41	1.40	...

Gini Coefficient (after tax and after transfers)

	1984	1985	1986	1987	1988	1989	1990	1991	1992	1993	1994	1995
Canada	0.36	0.36	0.36	0.36	0.36	0.35	0.35	0.36	0.36	0.35	...	...
Mexico	0.43	...	...	...	...	0.47	...	...	0.48	...	0.48	...
United States	0.40	0.41	0.43	0.41	0.41	0.42	0.41	0.41	0.42	0.43	0.43	...

Notes:

... = not available

For more information about data, see comparability and conceptual issues in Chapter IV.

[a] Minimum wage per hour in Canada and the United States; minimum wage per day for Mexico.

[b] For Canada, data are for all employees in the private sector excluding workers in agriculture, fishing, and trapping. For Mexico, data are for wage and salary workers in the private formal sector. For the United States, data are for full-time wage and salary workers in the private sector.

[c] For Mexico, data refer to wage and salary workers.

[d] Converted to U.S. dollars at commercial market exchange rate.

[e] Output per hour.

[f] Share of total family or individual income for Canada.

Sources: Canada, Statistics Canada, Survey of Employment, Payroll, and Hours and Survey of Consumer Finances; Mexico, Mexican Institute of Social Security, INEGI, National Income and Expenditure Survey; United States, Bureau of Labor Statistics, Current Population Survey.

Bibliography

AFL–CIO. "Workers' Compensation and Unemployment Insurance Under State Laws," Washington, D.C.: Author, 1996.

Akyeampong, Ernest B. "Working for the Minimum Wage." In *Perspectives*. Ottawa, Canada: Statistics Canada, Winter 1989: 8–19.

Anderson, Rolf. "Atlas of the American Economy: An Illustrated Guide to Industries and Trends." Washington, D.C.: Elliot & Clark Publishing, 1994.

Banco de México, Dirección de Organismos y Acuerdos Internacionales. "The Mexican Economy 1996." Mexico City, Mexico: Author, 1996.

Betcherman, G.; N. Leckie; and K. McMullen. *Developing Skills in the Canadian Workplace: The Results of the Ekos Workplace Training Survey.* Ottawa, Ontario: Canadian Policy Research Networks. Forthcoming.

Betcherman, G.; K. McMullen; N. Leckie; and C. Caron. *The Canadian Workplace in Transition.* Kingston, Ontario: IRC Press, Queen's University, 1996.

Bureau of National Affairs. *Benefit Costs and Practices.* Washington, D.C.: Author, 1995.

Canadian Policy Research Networks Inc. "Workplace Training Survey." Ottawa, Ontario: Author, 1996.

Cobble, D. S. "Making Postindustrial Unionism Possible." In *Restoring the Promise of American Labor Law.* Edited by S. Friedman, R. W. Hurd, R. A. Oswald, and R. L. Seeber. New York: ILR Press, 1994.

Comisión Nacional de los Salarios Mimimos. *Campendio de Indicadores de Empleo y Salarios.* Mexico City, Mexico: Author, December 1995.

Consejo Nacional de Población. "Proyecciones de Población Total y Económicamente Activa por Edad, ambos Sexos, 1996–2005." Unpublished.

Decima. "Decima Workplace Survey in Canada." Special survey. Decima, 1992.

European Commission. *Employment in Europe.* Luxembourg: Office for Official Publications of the European Communities, 1995.

Fleck, S., and C. Sorrentino. "Employment and Unemployment in Mexico's Labor Force." In *Monthly Labor Review*, pp. 3–31. Washington, D.C.: U.S. Department of Labor, November 1994.

Fuchs, V. R., and J. P. Jacobsen. "Employee Response to Compulsory Short-Time Work." *Industrial Relations* 30, no. 3 (1991): 501–13.

Human Resources Development Canada. "Adult Education and Training Survey." Ottawa, Ontario: Author, 1993.

———. "Employment Standards Legislation in Canada." Ottawa, Ontario: Author, 1995–1996.

———. *Report of the Advisory Group on Working Time and the Distribution of Work.* Ottawa, Ontario: Author, 1994.

———. *Statistics Canada Working Paper Series*, No. 71. Ottawa, Ontario: Author.

Human Resources Development Canada, Applied Research Branch. "Technological and Organizational Change and Labor Demand/Flexible Enterprise: Human Resource Implications." Ottawa, Ontario: Author, 1996.

Instituto Nacional de Estadistica Geografia e Informatica and the Ministry of Labor and Social Welfare. "National Survey of Employment, Salaries, Technology, and Training in the Manufacturing Sector." INEGI, STPS, 1992.

International Labor Organization. *World Employment 1995, An ILO Report.* Geneva: Author, 1995, 29, Table 4.

———. "Surveys of the Economically Active Population: Employment, Unemployment, and Underemployment." Geneva: Author.

Jusidman, Clara. "The Informal Sector in Mexico." Working paper no. 2. Mexico City, Mexico: Secretariat of Labor and Social Welfare in Mexico and the U.S. Department of Labor, 1993.

McMullen, K. *Skill and Employment Effects of Computer-Based Technology: The Results of the Working with Technology Survey, III.* Kingston, Ontario: Canadian Policy Research Networks Inc. Forthcoming.

Mexican Ministry of Labor and Social Welfare and the U.S. Department of Labor. "A Comparison of Labor Law in the United States and Mexico: An Overview." Mexico City, Mexico: Author, 1992.

Mishel, Lawrence, and Jared Bernstein. *The State of Working America, 1992–1993.* Economic Policy Institute Series. Armonk, N.Y.: M. E. Sharpe, 1993.

National Commission for Employment Policy based on University of Michigan's "Panel Study of Income Dynamics."

National Income and Expenditure Accounts. *Conference Board of Canada Compensation Planning Outlook*, 1996.

Organisation for Economic Co-operation and Development. "Employed and Unionized Workers in the Industrial Sector of the Federal Jurisdiction." STPS, March 1996.

———. *Employment Outlook.* Paris: Author, 1993, 1994, 1995, and 1996 (published annually).

———. *National Accounts, Main Aggregates*, Vol. 1.

———. *OECD Economic Surveys, Canada.* Paris: Author, 1995.

———. *OECD Economic Surveys, Mexico.* Paris: Author, 1995.

———. *OECD Economic Surveys, United States.* Paris: Author, 1995.

———. *OECD Education at a Glance.* Paris: Author, 1995.

———. *The OECD Jobs Study—Evidence and Explanations. Part I, Labor Market Trends and Underlying Forces of Change.* Paris: Author, 1994.

———. *The OECD Jobs Study—Evidence and Explanations. Part II, The Adjustment Potential of the Labor Market.* Paris: Author, 1994.

———. *The OECD Jobs Study—Evidence and Explanations: Employment in Europe.* European Commission. Paris, Author, 1995.

———. "Public Education Expenditure." *Costs and Financing: An Analysis of Trends, 1970–1988.* Paris: Author, 1995.

OECD and Statistics Canada. *Literacy, Economy, and Society; Results from the First International Adult Literacy Survey.* Paris: Author, 1995.

Pedrero, Mercedes. "Estado Actual de Las Estadísticas sobre Empleo en México." In *Cuadernos de Trabajo 4.* Mexico City, Mexico: Secretaría del Trabajo y Previsión Social, 1994.

Picot, G.; J. Baldwin; and R. Dupuy. "Working Paper Series 71." Ottawa, Ontario: Statistics Canada, 1994.

Poder Ejecutivo Federal. "Primer Informe de Gobierno, Anexo." Mexico City, Mexico: Subsecretaría de Egresos, de la Secretariat de Haciend y Credito Publico, 1995.

Rendón, Teresa, y Carlos Salas. "El Empleo en México en los Ochenta. Tendencias y Cambios." In *Comercio Exterior* 43, no. 8 (August 1993): 717–30.

Revenga, Ana, and Michelle Riboud. "Unemployment in Mexico: Analysis of Its Characteristics and Determinants." Washington, D.C.: World Bank, 1992.

Samaniego, Norma. "El Mercado de Trabajo Mexicano." Revista Mexicana del Trabajo, Nueva Epoca, no. 4/5. Mexico City, Mexico: Secretaría del Trabajo y Previsión Social, 1994.

Schor, J. B. *The Overworked American.* New York: HarperCollins, 1993.

Stambrook, David. "On-the-Job Training and Organizational Effectiveness." *Labor Force Development Review,* research report no. 6, Ottawa, Ontario: Canadian Labor Force Development Board, 1993.

Statistics Canada. *Aggregate Productivity Measures 1993,* Catalogue 15–204 E Annual. Ottawa, Ontario: Supply and Services Canada, 1995.

———. "General Social Survey and Labor Force Survey." Ottawa, Ontario: Supply and Services Canada.

———. *Income After Tax, Distributions by Size in Canada 1993.* Catalogue 13–210 Annual. Ottawa, Ontario: Supply and Services Canada, 1995.

———. *The Size of the Underground Economy in Canada.* Catalogue 13–603E. Ottawa, Ontario: Supply and Services Canada, 1994.

Statistics Canada, National Income and Expenditure Accounts. *Conference Board of Canada Compensation Planning Outlook.* Ottawa, Ontario: Supply and Services Canada, 1996.

Statistics Canada, National Income and Product Accounts. "National Childcare Survey." Ottawa, Ontario.

Stein, H., and M. Foss. *The American Economy.* Washington, D.C.: AEI Press, 1995.

USA Today Poll, 1995.

U.S. Chamber of Commerce. *Study of Employer's 1993 Benefit Costs.* Washington, D.C.: Author, 1994.

U.S. Department of Commerce, Bureau of the Census. "Money Income in the United States 1995." *Current Population Reports.* Washington, D.C.: Government Printing Office, September 1996.

U.S. Department of Labor. *International Labor Comparisons in G–7 Countries: A Chart Book.* Washington, D.C.: Government Printing Office, 1994.

———. "The Underground Economy in the United States." Occasional paper no. 2.

Secretariat of Labor and Social Welfare and U.S. Department of Labor, September 1992, pp. 16–17.

U.S. Department of Labor, Bureau of Labor Statistics. "How the Government Measures Unemployment." Report 864. Washington, D.C.: Government Printing Office, February 1994.

———. "International Comparisons of Manufacturing Productivity and Unit Labor Costs Trends, 1995." In *News*, 17 July 1996, Washington, D.C.: Author.

———. "Report on the American Workforce." Washington, D.C.: Government Printing Office, 1994, 1995 (published annually).

———. "Revisions in Current Population Survey, Effective January 1994." *Issues in Employment and Earnings*, February 1994.

———. "Supplement to the U.S. Current Population Survey." Washington, D.C.: Government Printing Office, February 1995.

———. "Survey of Employee Benefits in Small Establishments." Washington, D.C.: Government Printing Office, 1992.

———. "U.S. Current Population Survey." Washington, D.C.: Government Printing Office.

Weinberg, Daniel. "A Brief Look at Postwar U.S. Income Inequality." In *Current Population Reports*, Census Bureau, U.S. Department of Commerce. Washington, D.C.: Government Printing Office, June 1996.

The World Bank. "Workers in an Integrating World." In *World Development Report 1995*. New York: Oxford University Press, 1996.

Glossary

blue-collar occupations: processing, machining, construction, materials handling, transportation, and primary industries

discouraged workers: workers who have given up looking for work and are no longer considered in the labor force

disposable income: income after taxes and transfers

empleados de confianza: in Mexico, employees defined as "confidential," who could not become unionized

experienced unemployed workers: job losers, job leavers, and reentrants into the work force

formal training: training that is structured, is planned, and has a defined curriculum

formal sector: in Mexico, workers in enterprises registered with the IMSS

Gini coefficient: a summary measure of income inequality ranging from 0.0 when every household (family and unattached individual) has the same income, to 1.0 when a household (family and unattached individual) has all the income

government transfers: cash payments made to an individual or household

high-skill occupations: management, professional, and technical categories

hourly compensation costs: compensation costs per employee hour worked

incidence of unemployment: the percentage of people in the labor force who become unemployed in a given period

income: wages and salaries, net income from self-employment, investment income, government transfer payments, and miscellaneous income

informal sector: The concept of informality, defined as self-employment and workers in small economic units, was first used by the ILO in 1972 to analyze employment conditions in Kenya. Since then the concept has changed. In developing countries where the concept is mainly related to family subsistence criteria, informality is sometimes associated with the underground economy. In Mexico, it has different definitions. Here it refers to household domestic work; employees, employers, and piece workers in small establishments (excluding sectors usually defined as formal); and unpaid workers.

insurance employees: in Mexico, salaried permanent workers covered by the IMSS

involuntary part-time workers: workers who are able to find only part-time work

"just-in-time" production: when goods are produced just before they are needed by the customer

labor income: payments received from wages, salaries, and supplementary income

labor productivity: output per hour or employee

low-skill occupations: services categories

maquiladoras: in-bond industries located in national territory that establish a contract to process or assemble components and machinery temporarily imported and to re-export them thereafter. By 1988 the *maquiladoras* were allowed to sell a portion of their goods on the domestic market.

Medicaid: a term used to refer to a U.S. federal and state program of health insurance for the poor

Medicare: a term used to refer to a U.S. federal program that provides health care for those over 65 years of age

medium-skill occupations: clerical, sales, and blue-collar categories

nonstandard employment: includes part-time workers, "own-account" self-employed workers, temporary or contract workers, and multiple job holders

outsourcing: when a self-employed independent contractor sells all of his or her production services to a former employer

"own-account" worker: self-employed workers. In Mexico and Canada, the category includes both incorporated and unincorporated self-employed workers, whereas in the United States, it includes only unincorporated self-employed workers.

"passive" job hunters: those who read help-wanted ads but do not engage in job-seeking activity

primary sector: farming, forestry, trapping, and fishing

processing occupations: occupations related to the manufacturing sector including production, craft, repair, operators, fabricators, and laborers

purchasing power parities (PPPs): In comparing purchasing power of earnings, PPPs are given in national currency units per U.S. dollar to eliminate differences in price levels among countries.

salario base de cotización: in Mexico, the definition of basic earnings upon which contributions to the IMSS are made

SAR: in Mexico, retirement savings system

secondary sector: manufacturing, mining, and construction

sector, tertiary, or service: transportation, communications, utilities, community, business, and personal services, wholesale and retail trade and finance, insurance and real estate, and government services

Social Security: a term used to refer to a U.S. federal program that provides retirement income and death and disability benefits to workers

temporary workers: workers who expect their job will last for one year or less. The definition varies considerably by country and by whether or not self-employed workers, independent contractors, and wage and salary workers who have worked more than one year in the same job but do not expect their job to last are included in this category.

trabajadores a destajo: a growing category of piece workers in Mexico who are not susceptible to unionization other than through their occupation

unattached individual: a person living alone or in a household where he or she is not related to other household members

unincorporated self-employed workers: those who have not set up their business as a legal corporation

unit labor cost: ratio of labor compensation to real GDP, a measure of the cost of labor per unit of real output

welfare: a term used to refer to a U.S. federal program of general assistance for poor citizens with children

white-collar occupations: managerial, administrative, clerical, service, and sales

List of Abbreviations and Acronyms

AFORES: Administradoras de Fondos Para el Retiro de los Trabajadores

CALURA: a survey of labor unions in Canada

CES: Current Employment Statistics Survey (United States)

CONAPO: National Population Council (Mexico)

CPS: Current Population Survey (United States)

ECI: Employment Cost Index (United States)

ENE: National Employment Survey (Mexico)

ENIGH: National Income and Expenditure Survey (Mexico)

GDI: gross domestic investment

GDP: gross domestic product

ILO: International Labor Organization

IMSS: Mexican Institute for Social Security (Instituto Mexicano del Seguro Social)

INEGI: Instituto Nacional de Estadística Geografía e Informática (Mexico)

INFONAVIT: Instituto del Fondo Nacional de la Vivienda Para Los Trabajadores

ISSSTE: Institute for Security and Social Services for Public Servants (Mexico) (Instituto de Seguridad y Servicios Sociales de los Trabajadores del Estado)

LFS: Canadian Labor Force Survey

MIS: Monthly Industrial Survey (Mexico)

NAALC: North American Agreement on Labor Cooperation

NAFTA: North American Free Trade Agreement

OECD: Organisation for Economic Co-operation and Development

PPPs: Purchasing Power Parities

SCF: Survey of Consumer Finances (Canada)

SEPH: Survey of Employment, Payrolls, and Hours (Canada)

STPS: Ministry of Labor and Social Welfare (Mexico)